Singing
in the
WILDERNESS

Singing

in the
WILDERNESS

Let God forgive and heal the pain of your past.

Learn how to sing and see the joyful
opportunities in every aspect of your life.

Luana Stoltenberg

XULON PRESS

Xulon Press
2301 Lucien Way #415
Maitland, FL 32751
407.339.4217
www.xulonpress.com

Printed in the United States of America.

ISBN-13: 9781545617045

Endorsements

In this book, Luana offers freedom, forgiveness, and a hope for the future. She does it in the most gentle and powerful way. Through her own journey of the pain and shame in her past, she takes the reader to a new day filled with God's healing love.

Kathy Troccoli
Recording Artist, Author, Speaker

Luana Stoltenberg's story is the story of millions of women in America; however, she's had the courage to openly reveal that an abortion ends a life but not the pain and the guilt. Her story is deeply personal and told with depth and raw candor—nothing candy-coated in taking responsibility for decisions made or for the grace received. *Singing in the Wilderness* will take you through a journey of forgiveness, healing, and restoration. I invite you to sit before the Lord as you read this book and receive all Jesus has for you.

Mike Huckabee
Arkansas Governor (1996–2007), Author, TBN and Fox News Personality

I have watched Luana Stoltenberg grow over the years as she has become a true spokesperson for life, sharing her story with powerful and influential people. Now with *Singing in the Wilderness*, the unique aspect of Luana's work shines through as she interweaves her story with words of encouragement and prayers for her readers. She reaches out and imparts hope with a call to scriptural action.

Luana's heart for leading others to forgiveness and healing comes through in a combination of an autobiography and devotions—a valuable tool for anyone who has been affected by abortion or another traumatic experience. It will inspire you and others on a healing journey. I strongly recommend you read this special book and receive the love, compassion, and steps for continued healing that Luana offers in a deep and heartfelt way.

Carol Everett
Founder and CEO of The Heidi Group

Singing in the Wilderness is one of the most compelling and powerful books I have ever read. From the aching depths of sadness to the Song of the Redeemed. Who would not want that joy? Luana has lived—and lives—this message like no one I have ever known. Everyone needs to read this book.

Allan Parker
President of The Justice Foundation, Co-founder of Operation Outcry

Too many people are secretly suffering from hidden shame. Luana has carved a clear path for them to follow out of a place of darkness and into the light. *Singing in the Wilderness* is a perfect example of God taking your greatest pain and turning it into your most powerful prophecy.

I have had the honor of partnering with Luana for many years on initiatives around the country and on Capitol Hill. I count it a privilege to stand with her, pray with her, and watch God promote the message he has given her.

Matt Lockett
Director of Bound for Life

My prayer is that God will use this book to impact many lives for his kingdom. *Singing in the Wilderness* will open up to you the promises of God and the power of his love in a way that will bring comfort, encouragement, restoration, and rejoicing. No matter how deep your valley goes, Luana Stoltenberg brings an uplifting read to get you to your mountain top.

Pastor D Robinson
TBN's Director of Pastoral Care

Reading *Singing in the Wilderness*, I felt such a strong connection with Luana and found myself nodding my head in agreement with her words. Although we have lived out opposite ends of the abortion experience (Luana as a mother who had abortions and myself, a child who survived my birth mother's abortion), her struggles and suffering—and her triumphs and victories as she found God in the midst of it all—were familiar to me. No matter what your experience, God is present, healing, redeeming, restoring, and reconciling. May you find comfort and hope in Luana's story and the lessons she's learned on her journey which she is bravely sharing.

Melissa Ohden
Christian Speaker, Author of *You Carried Me: A Daughter's Memoir*

Luana's testimony of Jesus' life transformation and healing from abortion is fascinating and redemptive. Of the many books I've read with post-abortion recovery testimonies, Luana's is unique. Each chapter ends with thought-provoking questions designed for any reader to ponder or discuss in a small group. Those who've not personally experienced the tragedy of abortion will gain insight and be challenged with the soul-searching questions. Post-abortive women will identify with Luana and continue in their healing process.

Susan Skoglund
Executive Director of Pregnancy Resources (15 years)

This book is dedicated first to Jesus, my Lord and Savior. Without him, the only words written about me would be on my tombstone, not in this book. He is my God of life!

Also to my mom, dad, and my sister Linda, for their prayers and persistent witness of Jesus that brought me into his loving arms and eternal salvation.

Then to my husband, Steve, who is Jesus wrapped in skin to me. He is ever showing me grace, love, and the kindness of the Lord.

Next, to my son, Zac: You are our "precious gift from God." You have only added to our lives. To Zac's birth mom as well, for without your selfless sacrifice we would have a huge void and missed out on the treasure God had for us through Zac.

To Twila Belk, you have been there for me during this whole process. I could not have done this without you. I love you, friend

To Stacie Hoppman, thank you. I love you so much.

I also dedicate this book to all the amazing friends I consider precious pearls. You know who you are. It is the sacrificial time and wisdom you poured into me—mixed with God's love—that shaped me into a weapon and instrument for the kingdom of God.

I love you all.
Luana

Table of Contents

"The LORD will call you back as if you were a wife deserted and distressed in spirit—a wife who married young, only to be rejected," says your God. (Isaiah 54:6)

"Do not be afraid; you will not be put to shame. Do not fear disgrace; you will not be humiliated. You will forget the shame of your youth and remember no more the reproach of your widowhood." (Isaiah 54:4)

"For your Maker is your husband—the LORD Almighty is his name—the Holy One of Israel is your Redeemer; he is called the God of all the earth." (Isaiah 54:5)

"Sing, barren woman, you who never bore a child; burst into song, shout for joy, you who were never in labor; because more are the children of the desolate woman than of her who has a husband," says the LORD. (Isaiah 54:1)

"Now I have sworn not to be angry with you, never to rebuke you again. Though the mountains be shaken and the hills be removed, yet my unfailing love for you will not be shaken nor my covenant of peace be removed," says the LORD, who has compassion on you. (Isaiah 54:9–10)

"Afflicted city, lashed by storms and not comforted, I will rebuild you with stones of turquoise, your foundations with lapis lazuli." (Isaiah 54:11)

"All your children will be taught by the LORD, and great will be their peace. In righteousness you will be established." (Isaiah 54:13–14)

"See, it is I who created the blacksmith who fans the coals into flame and forges a weapon fit for its work. And it is I who have created the destroyer to wreak havoc." (Isaiah 54:16)

"Enlarge the place of your tent, stretch your tent curtains wide, do not hold back; lengthen your cords, strengthen your stakes." (Isaiah 54:2)

"For you will spread out to the right and to the left; your descendants will dispossess nations and settle in their desolate cities." (Isaiah 54:3)

"No weapon forged against you will prevail, and you will refute every tongue that accuses you. This is the heritage of the servants of the LORD, and this is their vindication from me," declares the LORD. (Isaiah 54:7)

Foreword

There is a quote from Ernest Hemmingway in his *A Farewell to Arms* that reads, "The world breaks everyone and after, many are strong at the broken places." I am honored to have met and befriended Luana, a woman broken by the world but whose strength shines forth from those broken places. Luana is a woman of passion, of fire, of laughter and joy—a woman who came forth from the wilderness singing words of life. She has been a source of inspiration to me, and I hope that her story similarly inspires you.

Throughout my political career and my run for president, I have had the opportunity to meet many people, but there are few like Luana. She has been a part of many pro-life groups and ministries, and our paths crossed as I was working on pro-life issues, legislation, and political campaigns. I noticed her passion and dedication.

When you hear Luana speak about her story and the stories of women impacted by abortion, you can see in her eyes the pain and the heartbreak, but also a hope that is never stifled or diminished. Her face lights up and she grows more animated as she shares with you how God is moving, how Christ is speaking, and what the future holds.

Luana never stops believing. She is a true woman of faith. Though she has suffered long in the wilderness, Luana does not allow the chains of that experience to hold her back or to bind her. Instead, she uses her past to fuel her present, to give life to her dreams and her story, and to inspire the song she sings. After reading *Singing in the Wilderness*, you can't help but walk away enamored with life and an innate sense of the way God values each and every one of us.

Initially, Luana's story brought tears to my eyes. I found myself swallowing the lump in my throat as I listened to the all-too-familiar tale of abandonment and feelings of worthlessness. How many people—men and women alike—walk through life feeling just like Luana did? How many of us have stories that mirror this search for true love everywhere but the arms of Jesus? How many times have we beaten ourselves up, feeling lost and unable to be saved? It's a story of battling the flames and getting burned, of fighting the waves until we're so tired we slip beneath the surface.

The beauty of Luana's story, what turns tears of sorrow to tears of joy, is that from the ashes emerges this picture of love that could only have been painted by God himself. What should have been forever lost has been found, has been rebuilt and washed white in the blood of Christ. This reality belongs to Luana, but it is not hers alone, and that is what is so wonderful about it. This story, Luana's story, has been written with the hope that so many others might find what she has. It has been written with the hope that those who even now are wandering in the wilderness will hear the voice of love and forgiveness calling them homeward.

First and foremost, valuing life begins with understanding the value of your own life in the eyes of God. Once you see yourself as a masterpiece—as a piece of clay that God the potter has molded and shaped, sometimes painfully but always with purpose—you can recognize that same value in those around you. As you read this book, I hope Luana's journey will help you to recognize your own worth and your own calling. I hope that you will be filled with passion to the same degree that my dear friend Luana is and that you will not allow the flames or the waves to overwhelm you. Though each of us has our broken places, in Christ we have the power to be stronger, to speak light to those who are still in darkness.

Singing in the Wilderness is a spotlight, a testament to the triumph of the cross of Christ in even the most hopeless of circumstances. Read it and remember that this triumph is not contained to one life, to one person, but open to all who lay their burdens down at the feet of Jesus.

Senator Rick Santorum
Attorney, Author, Politician, and CNN Political Commentator

Introduction

*L*ife. Who of us has it all figured out? It can be so wonderful at times and at others so difficult.

Most go through this human race trying to come out unscathed with no scars or pain, bank accounts full, fame and prestige, and wanting to say we are happy and successful. But I know of none so far who have accomplished that feat.

We will all face trials and triumphs, heartaches and love, and betrayals and devotions, but what will truly define our character and success is how we run our race.

The first thing we must understand is how much the Lord loves us. Everything we experience in this life will be filtered through that amazing love and will be for our benefit. He is a good God. There is NO thing in him that is not good. If we can know and comprehend that truth, we will look at matters from a different perspective.

When we grasp how much he cherishes us, we'll more easily sing in the wilderness and barren areas because we know who mapped out our course. His never-ending love and his desire for our best make it possible for us to trust him in those hard places.

Here are a few words to describe wilderness: any desolate, barren, or unpopulated area; uninhabited; wasteland; usually linked with danger; a position of disfavor.

How many times in your life have you felt you were in the wilderness? You struggle in that tough spot and feel as if you will never escape and find what you were destined for. You know that mountain top everyone wants to live on?

But some of our best times of learning are in our places of greatest pain and challenge.

A favorite Scripture passage of many is Psalm 23: "The Lord is my shepherd, I lack nothing. He makes me lie down in green pastures, he leads me beside quiet waters, he refreshes my soul. He guides me along the right paths for his name's sake. Even though I walk through the darkest valley, I will fear no evil, for you are with me; your rod and your staff, they comfort me. You prepare a table before me in the presence of my enemies. You anoint my head with oil; my cup overflows. Surely your goodness and love will follow me all the days of my life, and I will dwell in the house of the Lord forever."

I love this Psalm because it is so descriptive of our wilderness seasons. We learn he is always with us and will give us all we need in those times. He says to just lie down in the green pasture and he will carry us. He will lead us to the quiet place so he can restore our soul—if we let him. If we will be still in him and listen for his voice, trusting him to lead us through the hurt, brokenness, and heartache, he will use those fractured pieces of our life to create a beautiful vessel of honor. He never wants to harm us or destroy us. He wants to grow us in faith, wisdom, and righteousness so we will reflect him and bring glory to his name.

Even when we are in the valley of death, we can rejoice in the shadow, because shadows cannot exist without light. We need only to grab tight, hang on, and trust our shepherd. His rod of correction and staff of direction will comfort us. He's promised to set a table for us in front of our enemies; and he has big plans to throw a banquet for us and give us plenty, right under our enemy's noses. Yes, even in the dry places our cup can run over.

We're not especially fond of being in those valleys. We want to be on the mountain top, where we can look out and see the wonder and magnificent artistry surrounding us. But what we tend to forget is that nothing grows at the peak. In fact, there is no vegetation at all. Only rocks and dirt.

Isn't it interesting that all the waters and streams from the mountain flow down into the valley, creating the best conditions for abundant growth? The soil there is lush and fertile.

In a similar way, God can produce beautiful fruit in our lives during our valley experiences.

Once we accept the fact that he can shape us, prune us, and grow us in difficult situations, we need to learn to sing and dance along the way. Then we can enjoy the process and journey, allowing the pain to become passion and opportunity.

I was raised in a home where we knew about Jesus and how he died on the cross for our sins, but I never really understood what that meant. I didn't realize I could have a personal relationship with him as my Lord, Father, protector, comforter, and everything else he is to us.

My early years were lived from a place of insecurity and selfishness. I tried to find my own way, but I didn't do a good job. Most of those years I spent roaming through the wilderness, seeking an escape route.

In that wilderness I cried, blamed others, and looked for someone—anyone—who would love me, not knowing the One who loved me most was right there all along. I made horrible choices and sinned gravely against God. I was a fornicator, an adulterer, a murderer, a liar, and an alcohol and drug abuser. I was the worst of the worst. But in all of that, God still was so in love with me and wanted the best for me.

Because I took the path of disobedience in my life, I was left with deep wounds, destructive behavior, mistrust of others, and a brokenness that could not be repaired by anyone other than Jesus. Before I met him, I tried everything I could to get out of my messy wilderness.

I tried running from it and numbing myself in it. I even tried killing myself, but God had a better way. He is the way, the truth, and the life. He is the light I needed on my path to lead me out of that wilderness. He is the healer of my wounds, the restorer of my past, and the redeemer of my life. He is my all in all.

My prayer as you read this book is that you will come to know the One who intentionally created you in a deeper and more intimate way. That you will see those places of pain in your past as positions of passion to bring freedom to you and to others who have experienced similar pain. That you will see them as places where God wants to reveal himself and show you his faithfulness.

I pray you will go back to those places—not to find blame, or to stir old hurts and pain, but to go back while holding the hand of Jesus. You are seated with him in heavenly places, so now you can have a new perspective of the landscape of your life. You have the Word as your plumb line as well as your sword of truth, which enable you to see your past from a place of grace and truth.

Oh, dear one, even in the areas you made wrong choices and need to repent, the Lord has his arms of forgiveness wrapped around you. He says it is his kindness that leads us to see the sorrow of our sin, so we want to repent and be right with our Father.

I am excited about the journey you are on. In the journey there may be places of wilderness, but if you sing through them you will not come out the same. You will come out expanded, needing to enlarge your house, for you will be bursting at the seams. (See Isaiah 54:2–3.)

Remember, God is going with you. He goes before you, and he is your rear guard. He has only good things in store for you.

He says in Jeremiah 29:11–14, "For I know the plans I have for you," declares the LORD, "plans to prosper you and not to harm you, plans to give you hope and a future. Then you will call on me and come and pray to me, and I will listen to you. You will seek me and find me when you seek me with all your heart. I will be found by you," declares the LORD, "and will bring you back from captivity."

In Isaiah 54:11–14, the Lord says, "O storm-battered city, troubled and desolate! I will rebuild you with precious jewels and make your foundations from lapis lazuli. I will make your towers of sparkling rubies, your gates of shining gems, and your walls of precious stones. I will teach all your children, and they will enjoy great peace. You will be secure under a government that is just and fair. Your enemies will stay far away. You will live in peace" (NLT).

The Lord promises you he will rebuild you with beautiful gems. He doesn't see a pile of rubble but a valuable treasure. His promise is not only to rebuild you but also to train and teach your children, and generations to come. They will know him, and they can live in the peace of God that passes all their understanding and guards their hearts and minds. You and your generations will live under the government of the kingdom of God, so you can live in peace.

Oh, precious one, it is worth the pain of going back to the wilderness of our past so we can burst out with our cup overflowing, and with blessings, goodness, and unfailing love pursuing us all the days of our lives.

It will also help us in our upcoming days as we face wilderness times. We will have the experience and faith to know that as we sing and find joy in the trials, God will be faithful to turn them into opportunities. We will be like the oaks of righteousness in Isaiah 61:3 that are planted in good soil and bring glory to our wonderful God.

As I soar with the Lord and look down from heavenly places, I see his shining glory rising from the wilderness, and I hear a song of victory coming from you, precious child of God. I believe in you because I believe in him.

Come on, beloved, get on your mark, get set, and let's go! Let's run this race no matter where the course takes us. Let's run it with the One who loves us. And let's win!

Prologue

*W*hen I first came to know the Lord, my passion was prayer and reading his Word. I loved learning about him, including all that he is and his intentions for me.

One day at my parent's house, I lay on the bed in what used to be my bedroom. I had my Bible open to chapter 54 in the book of Isaiah and started reading it. But I paused as I came to verse 4. "Fear not; you will no longer live in shame," it said. "Don't be afraid; there is no more disgrace for you. You will no longer remember the shame of your youth" (NLT).

The words jumped off the page. It seemed as if I heard the Lord's audible voice speak to me. The more I read, the more I was convinced the Lord wrote this to me personally. I wanted to go back to the beginning of the chapter and see if my name was written there.

I ran downstairs, yelling for Mom—my excitement leading the way. Just like a kid who had found a hidden supply of candy, I couldn't get there fast enough to show her my new discovery. "What's wrong?" she shouted back from her seat at the kitchen table, the concern in her voice obvious.

"Listen to this, Mom." I read Isaiah 54 out loud. "I know God wrote that just for me!" My awe of God's love for me showed as I gushed about how he had personally given me that nugget.

Mom smiled. "God does speak to us directly through his Word. When the words jump off the page like that, it's called the rhema Word of God. He is breathing the Holy Spirit upon that Word so it will change and transform us."

She pointed out John 1:1 and 1:4, which says, "In the beginning the Word already existed. The Word was with God, and the Word was God. The Word gave life to everything that was created, and his life brought light to everyone" (NLT).

In the days after that, the Lord took me to Isaiah 54 often. Each time he did, the verses I read revealed more about me. Today, the words of Isaiah 54 are the threads that make up the tapestry of my life. I have also found my story in many other books of the Bible. Or, I should say, I have found his story in my life.

My heart's cry for you as you read my book is that you will also find your story woven through the pages of God's living Word—for God has written it with you in mind, and every answer for your life is found upon its pages. You see, it is Christ in you, the hope of glory.

1. Rejected

"The LORD will call you back as if you were a wife deserted and distressed in spirit—a wife who married young, only to be rejected," says your God. (Isaiah 54:6)

It's my wedding day! It's my wedding day! Oh dear, it's my wedding day. This is supposed to be the happiest day of my life. I should be excited, so why am I crying and afraid?

Those were my thoughts many years ago. I had just turned sixteen a couple of months earlier, and four months before my birthday I found out I was pregnant. My sweet sixteen wasn't so sweet.

It's not the way I pictured my wedding day or the news of my first child, or the rest of my life for that matter. I'm not sure how I got to that place, but it sure wasn't where I wanted to be at such a young age.

Nobody Loves Me

I was raised in a home with five siblings, for a total of eight in our family. Eight really was enough. Each of our names starts with the letter "L"—even our dog, Lady, who was named before we got her. With five girls and only one boy, poor Larry didn't get much bathroom time and took a lot of teasing. But he deserved some of it, because he got his own room while the rest of us had to cram into two.

As a child, I felt unloved and unwanted. Many times I'd pack my little blue suitcase and tell Mom, "Nobody loves me. I'm running away!" I sadly walked across our yard and went straight to Mrs. Bird, an elderly widow who lived in the cute brick house next door. After notifying Mom that I'd arrived, Mrs. Bird soothed me with her homemade chocolate chip cookies, milk, and plenty of attention—the kind of attention I craved.

I was sick a lot when growing up, which required multiple stays in the hospital. I got pneumonia when I was two and had it just about every year after that. Because it usually happened around my birthday in March, Dad would bring a large cake to the hospital. I couldn't eat it, but the nurses loved it. Easter was during that same time of year too, so I stored my Easter candy in a box until I was healthy enough to enjoy it. Of course, my siblings were mad because I had candy long after theirs was gone.

As a two-year-old in the hospital, I was too young to understand that I was there to get well and that Mom had to care for other children at home. I couldn't comprehend why she walked out the door and left me alone. Jumping up and down in the crib that imprisoned me, I cried uncontrollably. "Mommy, M-o-o-o-m-m-m-y-y-y, come back! Don't leave me!" When she didn't return, I became so hysterical that I threw up all over the bed and myself. I wondered what I had done wrong. At that time I didn't know the word *rejection*, but I sure knew the feeling.

Dad owned a bakery and worked late at night through the middle of the day, including every weekend. He slept during the day. We didn't see him much, and he rarely did family activities or ate meals with us.

Maybe all the illnesses, hospitalizations, and the absence of my father contributed to my feelings of rejection. I just know I desperately wanted to be loved.

Meeting My Husband

Our family's bakery and coffee shop were a big part of our lives, and Dad was proud to tell people I learned to walk on the wooden bench in the back room. Each of us siblings had our jobs and worked hard, but the fruit of our labor—the cookies, donuts, cakes, and pies—made it worthwhile. We filled up on Dad's delicious treats while we worked. That irritated Mom because we weren't hungry for dinner. But how could we resist? No one made breads and sweets like Dad.

Dad often hired our friends, and we made sure we had fun. The oven was the size of a small room. It had shelving designed like a Ferris wheel. When it wasn't in use, we climbed in and rode on the large rotating racks.

Huge aluminum mixing bowls, which Dad used for rising dough, sat on steel bases with wheels. For us they served as an exhilarating ride. One person would sit in the bowl while the other pushed, and we had races down the long aisle to see who could get to the back door first without tipping or crashing the bowls.

On Mondays, we cracked over thirty dozen eggs into five-gallon buckets. Occasionally some of those eggs found their way to the gas station windows next store. Yes, we were creative in the ways we entertained ourselves at work, but in case Dad is reading this, we'll save the rest of those stories for later.

The bakery is where I first met John[1]. It was summer, and we worked third shift together. He had an amazing sense of humor and made me laugh. A big practical jokester, he'd throw

---

[1] Not his real name

dough at me while I frosted donuts, and he loved sneaking up behind me and scaring me.

After our shift ended in the mornings, John often drove me home. Sometimes we took the quick route, which included the famous "airplane" hill. He would go so fast that the car became airborne and flew over the top of the hill. My stomach dropped as if we were on a carnival ride. Other times we went the long way home and spent the extra time talking.

I liked John and enjoyed being with him, but I wasn't sure how he felt about me. *He probably thinks I'm just a kid*, I thought. *After all, he's a senior in high school and I'm only a freshman.*

I soon learned how to capture his attention. While I walked to work in the afternoons, I passed his house, and if his car was in the driveway, I'd take the cigarette lighter. Once he got in and noticed it missing, he had to find me to get it back.

A few times I saw him drive by my house. One Saturday night he stopped to tell me his dog had run away. "I can help you look for him, if you'd like." Perhaps I said that a bit too eagerly, but John readily agreed. I jumped into his car and off we went. We searched for a while and eventually ended up at the park. He later admitted that he made up the lost-dog story so he could see me.

We walked around the pond and observed the goldfish swimming beneath the lily pads. We climbed the rock formations, looked out over the expanse of the mighty Mississippi River, and watched the huge barges come through the lock and dam. We swung high on the swings, shrieking as we felt our insides flip-flop. We chatted about school, work, and silly things that didn't even matter. We laughed and lay in the lush green grass looking up at the setting sun. I whispered, "Does it get any better than this?"

As we lay in the grass, John told me about his older brother who had been in the military and came home on leave. "We were so excited because we hadn't seen him for a long time," he said. "And then when he was home, he went out for a motor-cycle ride."

He was quiet for a few seconds before continuing. "He never returned." John's voice cracked as he told me about the accident that took his brother's life. "I didn't get to say good-bye. I asked God if my brother was in heaven, and when I looked up, a single raindrop landed on my cheek."

I hurt so badly for him, and my tears flowed freely. John had let me into a secret chamber of his heart. I longed to reach over and hold him, but I was too nervous. Instead, we silently watched as the beautiful stars began to appear and twinkle in the summer night's sky.

The moment was perfect, and that's when it happened—he turned and kissed me. My mind flooded with thoughts. What did this mean? Was this confirmation he liked me? I had never felt that way before, and it was wonderful.

Our special time quickly came to an end, though, because it was late and the park was closing. John drove me home. As we sat in the car saying goodbye, my magic moment transitioned into a heavy sense of fear. I hadn't told anyone where I was going, it was after 10:00 p.m., and my parents had strict rules. I knew that big trouble awaited me. Big. I wasn't allowed to date until I was sixteen years old, and I had just turned fourteen.

Tension at Home

Reality came crashing down as I looked out the window and saw Dad storming toward the car. He yanked the car door open and ordered John to go home. Then he grabbed me by the arm and yelled, "Get into the house, NOW!" He slammed the door shut so hard the whole car shook. As we marched up the steps that led to the house, Dad informed me that he would not tolerate my behavior and I had to find another place to live. Wow! That's a little extreme, I thought. Things had been tense around the house lately, but to kick me out for being late for curfew seemed pretty harsh.

I got a pit in my stomach and began to cry. I said I was sorry several times. I begged for another chance, and as I pleaded, he took my arm and directed me back down the concrete steps away from the house. Through my sobs I told him how overwhelmed I was with school, homework, and not having any free time because of the hours I worked at the bakery. I shared about the politics at work and how difficult it was on friendships.

Dad listened and admitted that he too was overwhelmed by the responsibilities he had. We walked around the block, enjoying the evening breeze and the sounds of the locusts in the trees. I sensed Dad's demeanor softening. Both of us appreciated the opportunity to unload the burdens we carried.

That was the first time I had a real conversation with my father. I saw Dad more as my boss and disciplinarian than as my father. I had a fear of him rather than a relationship. If we didn't do things a certain way by a certain time, we were punished.

Even though I was scared, I felt a connection with him and didn't want the walk to end. We circled the block, and once we were back in front of our house, Dad had calmed down. He turned and looked me in the eye. "I'll give you another chance. You can still live here, but things better change!" He said it sternly. I was relieved and promised him they would.

For me to remain at home, I had to follow the rules. What about my new relationship with John, though? Was I willing to take the risk to see him? I lay in bed thinking of the day's events and watched the reflection of the streetlight on the ceiling. Maybe it was all a dream. Doubts crept in. Why would John care about me? He was older and had more freedom to do what he wanted. Maybe he regretted kissing me and it wouldn't be a concern.

However, John didn't have regrets, and we continued to see each other. We had to be careful and very discreet, flying under my parents' radar, because as stressful as the atmosphere was at home, I had nowhere else to go and didn't want Dad to kick me out.

The anger and blame between my parents continued to intensify. I escaped the war zone by spending time at my friend Cindy's house, going for bike rides, and taking long walks. Mom felt Dad drank too much and spent more time in bars than with our family. Did she fear history repeating itself? Dad's father was an alcoholic and died at the age of forty-seven from cirrhosis of the liver, leaving Grandma to raise the youngest of their seven children alone.

In hopelessness, Mom admitted herself into the psychiatric ward of the hospital. Things changed dramatically. Lisa and Leslie were away at college, so Linda and I shared the responsibilities at home. We cooked meals, cleaned the house, and watched our siblings. We were expected to do all the added responsibilities as well as work at the bakery, do our homework, and visit Mom at the hospital.

In order to deal with the heartache and anxiety, I shared my hurts and concerns with John. He provided joy and a distraction from the stress and chaos around me. He helped me feel safe and loved, and we grew closer. Our physical relationship did as well.

We Are Having a Baby

Weeks later Mom was released from the hospital, and I learned I was pregnant. With the situation at home, I was afraid to tell my parents.

Cindy and I went for a walk to talk about my fears. Our steps took us up the gravel alley behind John's house. Just moments earlier he had told his parents I was pregnant. They were disappointed but supportive.

John saw us through the kitchen window and ran outside. He picked me up and spun me around. While I was in the air, he excitedly hollered, "Will you marry me?"

"Yes! Yes!" I was elated. My knight in shining armor had come to rescue me again.

We enlisted my older sisters to help tell my parents. The strategy was to be around the kitchen table when Mom and Dad came home on Saturday night, and we'd tell them together. Dad would be less likely to kill me if there were lots of witnesses. That was meant to be funny, but there was a measure of truth to it. My thoughts were that maybe with more people around he would control his temper.

When they arrived and saw us all, they immediately said, "What's wrong?"

Mom and Dad joined us at the table, and John got right to the point. "Luana's pregnant. We love each other and we're getting married." I was amazed at how John just blurted it out. Silence hung in the air as they processed the information. When Dad furrowed his brow, I thought it was over, but he remained calm.

Mom spoke first. "You're both too young to get married. You have your whole lives ahead of you. You can't go to school, work a job, and care for a child. You need to put the baby up for adoption." Dad suggested I stay with his sister who lived three hours away until the baby was born and placed for adoption. Of course, I would NOT be allowed to see John.

I sobbed and felt hopeless. Everyone was disappointed in me. I didn't want to live with strangers in another city while I was going through the hardest time in my life. How would I get through it, especially if I couldn't see John? My parents were choosing the best solution for them, but they didn't have a clue what I was going through or how I felt. Or at least that's what I thought.

I learned that wasn't quite true. Dad was fifteen years old when his father died. He couldn't finish high school because he had to get a job to help Grandma support their family. He didn't know what it was like to be pregnant at fifteen, but he was familiar with hopelessness, fear, rejection, and abandonment.

After abundant tears and much discussion, John and I went back to our original plan to get married and raise the baby. My parents reluctantly accepted our decision.

To be pregnant out of wedlock was not common in those days. People considered it shameful and looked down on girls in that condition. A single, high school teacher in my town got pregnant, and she lost her teaching position. Girls at my school who got pregnant disappeared for a while. Once they returned, everyone talked behind their back.

We had a lot to do—plan a wedding, find a place to live, furnish our home, and prepare for a baby. We rented a third floor apartment in a building Dad owned. Because it was only a couple of blocks from the bakery, I could walk to work while John had the car. On Saturdays we made deliveries for the bakery as payment for our rent. John kept his job at the parts store. I continued with school and planned to work at the bakery full-time during the summer. We set the wedding date for June sixth.

My emotions ran the gamut—up and down and everything in between. Sometimes I felt hopeful and looked forward to being married. Other times I cried as if my life was over. I wept over what I'd miss. No more hanging out with friends. No more going to proms, homecomings, and all the other things teenage girls do. I'd be a wife and soon-to-be mother, and my life was no longer about me.

The Wedding Day

We moved forward with the wedding plans, yet I was conflicted. Wasn't this supposed to be the best time of my life? Every girl dreams of her special day—the day she walks down the aisle in a magnificent gown, heading toward the man of her dreams. She meticulously works out all the details. She spends hours on the guest list, making sure no one is left out. She writes down the names of close friends to include as bridesmaids and dreams of the fun they'll have picking out the dresses they'll wear. She imagines how magnificent the room will look, from the color of the flowers and decorations to each glittering light and candle. Everything must be breathtaking and flawless.

I had ideas for our wedding, but that didn't matter. My parents made the plans. They scheduled it on a Sunday at their friend's restaurant. Because they didn't think the marriage would last, they booked a justice of the peace. I would wear the wedding dress my cousin Carol wore a few years prior. Dad would make the cake, and he and the restaurant would cater the food.

Although I was grateful for everything they were doing, it wasn't how I imagined my wedding day. I wanted to plan the details and enjoy the excitement of the occasion. We needed two witnesses, so I did get to make one decision—to ask my sister Leslie to be my maid of honor. Leslie wore a floor-length pink and brown striped dress that she had in her closet.

The wedding day arrived. It was warm, and lots of gray clouds filled the sky, but the sun peaked through from time to time. How appropriate, I thought. My mood was gray, but glimmers of joy and hope pushed through periodically. Many relatives attended, and a few friends from school. The ceremony took only about ten minutes. We kissed at the end, and I was a new bride at the age of sixteen.

Dad did an exquisite job on the cake. A bridge joined together two three-layer cakes, and a fountain rested between the bases. The purple roses and fountain water matched the ribbon that ran through my borrowed dress. We didn't have decorations or candles—the only flowers were the bouquets and boutonnieres of the wedding party.

A two-man band played music at the reception as guests danced. My eighty-year-old great uncle Greg was cutting a rug with my sisters and other young ladies who were awed with his dancing abilities. (He took professional dance lessons at Arthur

Murray's, and it showed.) Overall, the mood was joyful and the day went well.

Rock-a-bye Baby

To get our apartment ready to live in after we were married, our families worked together to fix it up and paint it. They furnished our new home with chairs, a couch, a bed, and a dresser they no longer needed. Dad supplied a small round table and two chairs for our kitchen from the coffee shop at the bakery. Mom and my sisters moved it all in and decorated each room. What a nice surprise to welcome us home after we returned from our three-day honeymoon!

The apartment had four rooms. Two tall, beautiful wood columns on each side separated the living and dining rooms. They were my favorite part of the apartment. The back door led to a large deck outside and stairs that went down to where we parked our car. I enjoyed warm summer evenings sitting on the deck, listening to the passing traffic and locusts screaming their songs. At three floors up, the stars seemed closer and brighter, and the concerns of the world and life seemed farther away.

Less than two weeks after our wedding day, I felt sharp pains in my abdomen as I worked at the bakery. I had experienced that before, but Mom told me it was false labor and not to worry. She suggested I get more rest. However, this time the pain continued to get worse, so I lay on the wooden bench, hoping it would subside. It wasn't time for the baby to come—I was only seven months along.

I called John to tell him about the pains and had barely hung up the phone when he rushed through the front door. He whisked me outside and into the front seat of the car that he had double-parked on the busy street. Then he sped to the hospital.

At that time, John's mom, Ann[2], was head nurse of the OB-GYN department at the hospital. John called to let her know we were on the way and asked her to meet us there. The pains kept getting more intense and closer together. As soon as we arrived, they put me in a room, and a nurse gave me an injection to relieve the pain. Flailing and fitful from the contractions, I wondered what was happening. It was too early for the baby to come, but I wanted to push.

John was not allowed in the delivery room, so Ann stayed by my side. She stroked my hair and wiped my forehead with a damp cloth, assuring me things would be okay. She told me when to push and when to stop. I was grateful to have her help and comfort. "Has anyone called my parents? Is Mom here?" I asked. Surely they wanted to see their first grandchild.

The room bustled with activity. Medical personnel shouted orders. Nurses came and went. And with one final push, the baby came out. Instantly, stillness filled the room. One of the nurses grabbed the baby and quickly carried her away. No one said a word to me, but their hushed whispers and body language signaled that something was wrong.

As new activity happened, my brain started to feel fuzzy, and exhaustion overcame me. I dozed in and out. The drug they gave me was obviously at work. Nurses transferred me to a different bed and moved me to a new room.

I must have fallen into a deep sleep, because when I awakened, John and Ann were by my side. It seemed as if they had been there awhile. They were crying and having a serious discussion. I asked what was wrong and if they had seen the baby. Ann slid her chair closer and held my hand. "You had a little girl," she said with tenderness, "but she was born dead. We named her Mary, and she will be buried in the baby cemetery down the street. Don't worry about the arrangements. We will take care of everything."

---

[2] Not her real name

Sadness came over me, yet I wasn't surprised. For some reason, I had never pictured life with this little girl. I hadn't bonded with her or felt her move. We hadn't even picked out names. I grieved that I didn't get to see her or know her.

I thanked Ann for her kindness and love and for taking care of everything. Although I was relieved and grateful that arrangements were made, it hurt me to not be included. Again, others made the decisions and we didn't have a say about our desires. Maybe they felt we were overwhelmed and just wanted to help.

I didn't want to cry or seem ungrateful, so I tried my best to hide my unstable emotions. I really wanted to see my mom, to have her hold me and tell me it would be all right. But my parents still weren't there. Mom didn't drive and Dad was working. Did they know their granddaughter had died? Did they care? I felt rejected again.

The next morning the nurse directed me to take a shower. When I stepped into the shower and felt the warm, refreshing water hit my face, I was still a bit dazed. I hadn't noticed that I forgot to remove my bra. I took it off and saw blood stains in the back. The front was wet with milk. And then it hit me that I just gave birth to a baby, but I was leaving the hospital without her because she was dead.

I hadn't cried over losing Mary; it hadn't sunk in. That moment awakened me to a new reality—I got married because of my pregnancy, and now the baby is gone. Questions flooded my mind. Will John still want to be married? Did he love me for me, or did he marry me to do the "right thing?" Will John reject me since there isn't a baby?

John assured me he loved me, and not much changed after I came home from the hospital. We hadn't decorated a nursery or collected baby clothes, toys, or other baby items, so there were no reminders of little Mary around. Both of us were sad, but neither of us knew how to handle it, so we just didn't talk about it.

The Death of Many Things

John and I continued making bakery deliveries on Saturdays to pay for our rent. I loved walking to work early Saturday mornings while it was still dark and smelling the fresh-baked-bread aroma from blocks away. In the winter I had a special routine. Once I arrived, I grabbed a carton of chocolate milk from the refrigerator and threw it in the cold snow. After that, I loaded the truck with the deliveries. Then I generously frosted a warm donut right out of the fryer and pulled my milk from the snow. Nothing is better than ice-cold chocolate milk with a fresh warm donut. That was a treat I looked forward to, especially since things at home weren't so good anymore.

John lost his job at the parts store and was looking for another one—a sore subject because we were struggling financially. And we still hadn't figured out how to do the marriage thing. Our age differences caused problems. John was old enough to drink and I wasn't. That meant we had our own friends and different lives. John had already graduated, and his friends worked jobs and hung out at the bars. I was looking at going back to high school for my junior year. My friends talked about boys they liked and colleges they were considering.

Young and immature, John and I had no life experiences to draw from to get us through that time. As the days passed, we drifted apart and began to live separate lives. We fought over silly, stupid things, but also about finances, keeping a job, and going out with friends. Tensions escalated, and neither of us was willing to change. We both gave up even trying. John didn't seem to desire me anymore, so I started spending time with a guy who worked at the gas station next to the bakery.

Shortly after our one year anniversary, we pulled the plug on any life that was left in our marriage. We cared for one another but didn't know how to be married without hurting each other.

Mom accompanied me to the divorce proceedings. I stepped into the witness box, and the judge asked, "Do you believe this marriage is irreconcilable?" I wasn't sure. I looked over at John. He nodded his head, so I said yes. The judge pounded his gavel on the desk—and with a bang, the divorce was final. I signed the papers, took back my maiden name, and the life I knew was over.

Was I rejected again or had I rejected John?

The Lie of Feeling Unloved and Rejected

Rejection is something we all experience in life. Even Jesus experienced it.

Isaiah 53:3 says, "He was despised and rejected—a man of sorrows, acquainted with deepest grief. We turned our backs on him and looked the other way. He was despised, and we did not care" (NLT).

Rejection is a spirit that wants us to feel unloved by God and others. When we are not walking in love, we will not be all God created us to be. John 3:16 tells us that God so loved the world he sent his only Son to die so we could be saved. LOVE SAVED US. If the enemy can get us to believe we are not loved, and are unworthy and rejected, we will never believe we deserve the amazing plan God has for our life.

Most of our feelings of rejection are a lie. We might get hurt from others who were hurt, or we misunderstand the situation and don't have the right perspective. The enemy comes and tells us, "They meant to hurt you and leave you out."

It's not true. When we believe and agree with that lie, it influences our life. We respond out of insecurity. We think others see us differently from the way they do. We build walls to protect ourselves from being hurt and rejected again. What really happens is that we prevent people from loving us when we hide behind our walls. We send the message, "I will reject you before you have the chance to reject me." We self-destruct and blame others for our hurts, when we are really the one pushing them away.

Here's truth: the Lord will never reject you. "For the LORD will not forsake his people; he will not abandon his heritage" (Psalm 94:14 ESV).

When you feel unloved or hurt by others, it is the enemy trying to isolate you and cause you to turn from the very ones who love you most. Run to Jesus and know that he is always there for you. He will bring you back to the place of truth. He is faithful even when we are not.

Psalm 34:17–19 says, "When the righteous cry for help, the LORD hears and delivers them out of all their troubles. The LORD is near to the brokenhearted and saves the crushed in spirit. Many are the afflictions of the righteous, but the LORD delivers him out of them all" (ESV).

§

Questions to Ponder

What are some of the things in your life that have made you feel unloved or rejected?

Are there hurts that come up over and over? Ask God to help you forgive those involved.

Ask the Lord if feelings of rejection are keeping you from being all he wants you to be.

Remember that God will never reject you. He loves you and came to die for you so he never has to be without you. He is ever calling you to himself.

I invite you to sit before the Lord with these questions and pray the prayer below. Ask him to show you where the roots of rejection came into your life and where you agreed with the lie the enemy told you.

Take authority over that spirit of abandonment and rejection. Declare the Scriptures above over the situation and your life. Hide the Word in your heart, getting it deep into your belief system. The more you speak the Word, the more you will believe it, receive it, and live in victory. Romans 10:17 says, "So then faith *comes* by hearing, and hearing by the word of God" (NKJV). Hearing the Word of God produces faith, and that faith produces life.

§

Prayer

Father, we come before you asking for forgiveness for all the places we have believed and agreed with the spirit of rejection. We ask you to destroy the power of the lies that have been over our life, and we annul the agreement we made with rejection. We give you permission to break down the walls we built. We declare, Lord, that you love us with an everlasting love. You protect us. You are our strong tower that defends us. We are hidden in the secret place of the Most High God.

Now, Lord, we come into agreement with what you say about us. We are your beloved. We are the head and not the tail. We are more than conquerors in Christ Jesus. You didn't reject us but adopted us as your own children. We are always victorious in you.

Lord, I ask you to hold each one who prayed this. Put them in your lap and let their foundation be built on the great love you have for them. Destroy the mindsets and lies of the enemy over their lives. Lord, fill those void places with your love and truth so each one of these will believe every word you have said about them. In Jesus' name, amen.

2. Shamed

"Do not be afraid; you will not be put to shame. Do not fear disgrace; you will not be humiliated. You will forget the shame of your youth and remember no more the reproach of your widowhood." (Isaiah 54:4)

Oh, rejection and unworthiness, where are you leading me? Will I follow you into shame and regret?

After the divorce I found freedom, or I tried to convince myself of that. It wasn't long before I was in another relationship. If only I had known the traps and snares on the path ahead! I had no worth or value and didn't love myself. When you don't love yourself, it's hard to love others. I thought that if I could please my boyfriend and give him what he wanted, I would earn his love. So that's exactly what I did. I gave myself away.

I heard a quote once that said, "Men give love to get sex, and women give sex to get love." It was true in my life. My definition of love was destroying me. The more of myself I gave away, the less of me there was. Love is kind. Love covers and protects. Love does not demand its own way. Love does not take or destroy. Oh, what a web of deception the enemy was weaving! He lured me into his trap, and I believed it all.

I took birth control pills and thought I had it all figured out. Obviously I didn't, because I got pregnant. How could that happen? There I was again—my life out of control and in crisis. I didn't know what to do. How would I tell my parents and family that I messed up again? I couldn't face disappointing them and admitting my failure. Fear filled me.

I weighed my options. My boyfriend had cheated on me many times. He slept with two other girls consistently, and it was a source of contention in our relationship. I cared about him, though, and thought that if I tried harder he might change. I was insecure and had no self-worth. Because of his unfaithfulness, getting married didn't sound like a good idea. What if he continued to cheat on me? Then I'd be divorced twice. What if he didn't want to marry me?

I could keep the baby, but turmoil ruled my life—not a good environment to raise a child. And I was afraid to do it by myself. Fear is a horrible companion. It takes over your thoughts, steals your dreams, paralyzes you, and deceives you. It also causes you to do things you wouldn't ordinarily do so you can feel safe or comfortable. In my fear, confusion, and indecisiveness, I went to a friend for advice.

My friend encouraged me to have an abortion. She said, "It's quick and easy, and no one has to know." She had one, was familiar with the process, and could help me. It seemed too easy. Could everything she said be true? You go into this clinic and a couple hours later you walk out like nothing happened? She convinced me to check into it. I wanted to talk to my boyfriend first, because he deserved to be part of the decision.

The "Choice"

My boyfriend left no doubt that he wanted me to abort. He had no desire to get married and definitely didn't want a baby. He said, "I think you should get an abortion, but you decide." He didn't say, "I love you. We can do this together." Clearly, he didn't plan on helping. If I kept the child, I'd need to do everything alone. It became a trade-off—either my relationship with him or the baby. He made it sound as if I could make the decision, but was it really my choice?

In came rejection. I thought he loved me, but he appeared to be rejecting me for "loving" him and was punishing me for the outcome. I made the painstaking decision, but because of the path I was on, I filtered the final outcome through my selfish fears.

With my boyfriend's persuasion and stamp of approval, I scheduled the appointment for an abortion. Together, we made the hour-and-a-half trip to the abortion facility. I was already scared, but my anxiety seemed to increase with every mile. We checked in at the front desk, and they gave me several forms to fill out. As I sat in the chair with the clipboard on my lap, I looked around at the other girls in the waiting room and noticed their fidgeting. Some rocked. Others shook their legs. I tried to ignore the nervous tension in the atmosphere so I could focus on getting the paperwork completed.

A clinic employee called my name and took me to a room in the back. Then a woman dressed in a nurse's uniform came in to ask me questions. Abortion had been legal only a few years, so she asked about my understanding of my decision and how I felt. She said I was ten or eleven weeks pregnant, according to the dates of my last period.

She answered every concern I had. "Is it a baby?" I asked.

"No, it's just a blob of tissue." She drew a dot on a piece of paper with her pencil. "It's a small clump of cells this size," she assured me.

"Will I feel pain?"

"No. It will be uncomfortable, and you will feel tugging and slight cramping, but it will last only a few minutes. It's quick and easy—even safer than carrying to term." She stated that as if it were a fact.

We didn't talk about anesthetics or pain medication. She acted like it was no big deal. She was the adult and medical expert, and I was just a teenager, so I believed her.

The nurse said the procedure took only about fifteen minutes, and when they finished I'd be taken to a room to recover. They wanted to observe me for about forty minutes. If all was well, they'd release me.

I signed the permission form, and we walked to a smaller room. She pointed me to the exam table. I stepped up and sat down. While she silently wrote on the papers she had carried in with her, I looked around the room and nervously picked at my fingers.

Dingy gray walls. Pictures taped to the ceiling. A tray of metal instruments at the foot of the exam table, along with an unfamiliar-looking machine. It was a typical exam room, like many I'd been in before, but this time my stomach was doing flip-flops. The nurse finished her paperwork and handed me a hospital gown and a folded paper sheet. "Change into the gown and get on the table. The doctor will be in shortly." She walked out and closed the door behind her.

The Abortion Procedure

Apprehensively, I stepped down off the exam table and almost fell. I steadied myself by leaning against it to undress, and put on the gown. I folded my clothes neatly, set them on the chair, and climbed back up on that cold surface with the paper sheet wrapped around me, terrified about what came next. I hadn't met the doctor. I didn't even know his name.

The door opened, and the nurse came in with the doctor following behind. "Are you ready?" she asked before telling me to lie down. Out came the stirrups. She tapped my leg to let me know my feet needed to find their place in them. Without saying a word to me, the doctor put on his gloves and did a visual inventory, making sure the instruments were in place.

No introduction. No questions. He didn't even look at me. He conversed with the nurse but not with me. I wondered if he realized I was in the room. *Maybe his silent treatment is punishment for my bad behavior. Maybe he's angry that he has to clean up my mess.*

Finally he said something. "You need to scoot down on the table a bit." I moved for him and he performed a physical exam to confirm I was pregnant.

Planned Parenthood says the decision for abortion should be between a woman and "her" doctor. Most abortions are done in stand-alone facilities by doctors who have NEVER met the women they perform the surgery on. They won't discuss the best options or even the procedure with her. They won't give her ALL the information so she can make an educated decision. It's not a choice—it's a lie sold to scared, vulnerable, desperate women who are looking for help. To the abortion industry, she is nothing more than a number and a dollar amount.

The doctor began a process to dilate my cervix muscle. One at a time, he systematically inserted different sized metal rods—called dilators—into my cervix. He started with a small one and continued to increase the size until my opening was large enough to insert the suction catheter. It was extremely painful, especially with no anesthetic.

When a woman goes into labor, her cervix naturally opens to allow the baby to pass through. But with an abortion, the physician manually and unnaturally dilates the cervix muscle, causing it to weaken. Because of that process, women who have had abortions are at higher risk to miscarry future pregnancies.

Once my cervix was wide enough, the doctor inserted a suction catheter and curette, which is a hollow plastic tube with a sharp, spoon-shaped instrument attached to one end. The base of the catheter attached to long tubing that connected to a jar. It was powered by a suction pump. "Relax," the nurse said. "You might feel some slight cramping for a few minutes."

When the doctor turned on the suction machine I heard a loud noise. And then came a severe tugging sensation. It was intrusive and accompanied by relentless, excruciating pain. My body tensed, and I gripped the sides of the table so hard my knuckles turned white. I tried staring at the ceiling. The pictures of the ocean and flowers taped there didn't even begin to distract me from my agony. Everything within me trembled. I fought to keep my body steady.

I turned my head to the right and noticed a jar there. Red blood exploded and splattered the sides. I wondered what was inside of it. Something passed through that seemed like more than just a clump of cells or a blob of tissue. Had I seen parts of a baby? Was it my baby? Were its arms and legs in there?

I strained to lift my head to look. The nurse pushed me back down. "Lie still," she said. My heart pounded. I didn't want to lie still; I wanted to see if it was my baby. Again, she pushed me down—this time with force. "I said lie down." Her voice was firm. Had I made a terrible mistake?

The pain intensified, at times to the point of unbearable. I tried to hold back the tears, but they streamed down my cheeks and into my ears. I strained again to see what was in the jar. The suction became more labored as a large piece (or part) passed through the catheter. It sounded like my vacuum at home when I accidently suck up the rug or a lone sock. My mind reeled. If it was just a dot like the nurse drew on the paper, then what was going into the jar?

The few minutes it was supposed to last seemed to take forever, and every muscle in my body hurt from being tensed. I wanted it to end. And they were wrong about the "slight" tugging and cramping!

It's Finally Over, Or Is It?

Finally the procedure ended. The nurse quickly wheeled the jar out of the room, shielding it with her body so I couldn't see. The doctor got up from his stool, took off his gloves, and walked out of the room, not saying a word to me. I felt dirty and worthless, as if I were a piece of trash that bothered them. This couldn't be right. I was relieved the physical pain was over, but a different kind of pain replaced it—an overwhelming sense of guilt and shame from what I had just done.

I know now that my baby was in that jar. At eleven weeks she had a heartbeat and brainwaves. All her organs were functioning, and she had toes and fingers—and even finger nails! She could squint and swallow. She was NOT a blob of tissue.

The nurse came back in and gave me aftercare instructions and a pad. "You need to take it easy for the entire day and rest," she said. "After you're dressed, I'll take you to another room." She walked out, and finally I could relax my body. I lay on the table like a limp rag.

I tried to get up, but I couldn't stop shaking. As I placed my unstable legs one at a time on the floor, I wasn't sure they would hold me. I took a few deep breaths, whispered to myself, "Calm down, Luana. You can do this," and stood to my feet. My weakness, light-headedness, and nauseated stomach reminded me that my body had been beaten and battered into trauma.

Barely able to stand to put on my clothes, I haltingly walked to the chair and sat while I finished getting dressed. I took more deep breaths in an attempt to collect myself, but it didn't work. All I wanted to do was break down and cry. They said it wouldn't hurt and would take only a few minutes. That was a lie. What else was a lie?

The nurse came in and took me to a room where other girls were sitting in recliners. "Help yourself to juice and cookies," she said and pointed to a tray on the counter. "If you feel better in about forty minutes, you can go home."

A sense of heaviness and oppression filled the room. Other than occasional sobs from some of the girls, it was quiet. No happiness. No excitement. Just people who couldn't even bear to talk or look at each other. Guilt does that. I felt awkward and uncomfortable, and from the looks of the others, they did too.

I fitfully reclined in the chair as thoughts of the procedure tormented my mind. I had an overwhelming urge to run as fast as I could—anything to distance myself from the mental agony I had created.

In the midst of the pain and distress, though, part of me felt relief, thankful it was over. I didn't have to feel the shame of telling everyone I was pregnant again. I didn't have to feel their disappointment. No one had to know my secret.

But had I just exchanged one secret for another and picked up more shame? Trust me, I didn't plan on telling anyone about what I had done.

My boyfriend sat next to me as we waited in silence. A couple of times he asked how I felt. "Fine," I said quietly. I was glad he was with me, but I was also angry and hurt. If I hadn't restrained myself, I would have yelled, "You have no idea what I just went through. Why are you acting like nothing happened and it was no big deal? Why didn't you protect me? Why didn't you fight for our baby and for us as a couple?" I had so many swirling emotions, and I longed to run away like I did when I was a child.

After a while the nurse came to check on me. "I'm fine," I said. "I want to go home." She gave me a tiny pill to help my cervix shrink back to its normal size. I swallowed it, signed some paperwork, and that was that. We walked out the door and headed back to our messed up life.

More Bad Choices

Conversation on the drive home was nonexistent except for a few brief comments. Rather than talk, I cried. My body continued to shake, and I still experienced the pain and cramping. As it became worse, I lay in the back seat of the car, curled into a ball. I bled heavily, and we had to stop a couple of times so I could change my soaked-through pads.

When we arrived home, I was still bleeding profusely. I knew something was terribly wrong, and I thought I was dying. I called the abortion facility to ask what I should do to alleviate the pain and bleeding. "I'm sorry, but you're not our problem anymore. You'll need to call your physician or go to the emergency room," the voice at the other end of the line said. She hung up before I could say anything else.

What just happened? I wasn't going to call anyone because it was my secret. The only doctor I ever went to was with my mom, and I definitely would not contact him. My parents— or anyone else for that matter—couldn't find out about this. I decided that if I bled to death, I deserved it for what I did. I took some ibuprofen for the pain and went to bed. I fell asleep not caring if I woke up the next morning.

I did wake up, but I had changed. Not only was my baby dead, but a part of me died with her as well. How could I be the same after that? Depression, grief, guilt, and shame overpowered me. I cried often and asked God, "Why is this happening to me?" I didn't realize my own bad choices had created the trouble in my life. I thought about killing myself so the sadness and pain could end. That way I'd no longer be a bother and disappointment to others.

I desperately wanted to be loved and protected, but with rejection from my boyfriend's unfaithfulness, and guilt and shame from the abortion, our relationship ended. I started over, but this time I had less hope and more fear.

The spirit of shame, death, rejection, and abandonment stalked me. I hated what I had done and become. I tried to run away by moving to a different city, but it followed me. Numbing myself so I couldn't feel became my only way to cope.

I drank and took drugs, and my behavior became even more destructive. My self-hatred furthered my promiscuity. I believed that no one would love me unless I gave myself to them. Maybe I could earn their love, I thought. But even then I didn't deserve it because of everything I had done wrong.

I was in a vicious cycle of being used and abused by men for so long that I didn't see the destruction it caused me. That was my way of life. I got pregnant two more times, and with both pregnancies we chose abortion. I say we because the men wanted nothing to do with a child or a marriage commitment.

I have vague memories of those two abortions. They're mostly a blur.

What I do recall is that my second abortion happened in an old, converted, two-story house in the college town where I lived. I walked in the front door to the living room that had become the waiting area. A young girl in jeans—a college student—came around the corner and handed me a clipboard. None of the employees wore medical uniforms. They had dreadlocks in their hair and sported tie-dyed shirts and jeans. Was I in the right place?

Their laid-back, no-care attitude matched their style. They did the procedure in a tiny, converted, upstairs bedroom that had dim lighting and old flowered wallpaper. The technique and pain were the same, but I learned to numb myself to everything around me. I was there physically and that was all.

My third abortion took place in that same college town, although I had moved to a city an hour away. Because of my shame, I used my friend's name rather than my own. They didn't ask for identification, so I didn't think it was a big deal. It never occurred to me what would have happened if there was a complication or if I bled to death. Whom would they have called? Would my parents have ever found out I died, or would I still be a missing person today?

That path spiraled me down into a deep, dark pit, and I had no clue how to find the way out. The drugs got harder, the drinking became heavier, the self-hatred grew deeper, and I attempted suicide three times.

On each occasion I tried to kill myself, the Lord spared me. One time I turned on the gas in the oven and laid my head on the door, waiting to die. I had just dozed off when a friend banged on the front door. I jumped up, turned off the gas, and ran out the back way so she wouldn't see me. As I sat on a swing at the park, I cried and said to myself, "What's wrong with you, Luana? You can't even do that right!" Little did I know that God had a plan for my life.

Why So Many Bad Choices?

Many people ask why I had two more abortions, especially after my first horrible experience. It's a good question, and one that I've asked myself. I believe it's the same question an alcoholic asks when he is taking that next drink. Or the drug addict when he is shooting up again. Or the wife or girlfriend who is being beaten for the umpteenth time and chooses to stay in that abusive relationship. None of them wants to live in the bondage of sin.

I was deceived and trapped in sin, not knowing how to get free. So, as Proverbs 26:11 says, I kept returning to my vomit. The definition of insanity is to keep doing the same thing over and over, hoping for different results. To get a clearer picture of what happens, imagine someone trapped in a room. He's handcuffed and blindfolded. Because he can't see or free himself from his shackles, he can't find the way out, so he struggles and fights. Eventually, he hopelessly gives up.

Second Corinthians 4:4 explains it this way: "Satan, who is the god of this world, has blinded the minds of those who don't believe. They are unable to see the glorious light of the Good News. They don't understand this message about the glory of Christ, who is the exact likeness of God" (NLT).

Hopelessness and self-destruction imprisoned me, and I didn't have the key to get out. Jesus is that key, but I didn't know him, nor did I think I was worthy of his love or forgiveness.

Proverbs 13:12 says, "Hope deferred makes the heart sick, but a dream fulfilled is a tree of life" (NLT). I had no hope, so my heart was sick. My longing to be loved was not fulfilled.

When I allowed the abortions in my life, I opened a door to the spirit of death. I didn't know the Lord or realize the truth. I didn't know how to close that door and annul the covenant I made with death. My life kept spinning out of control. I made bad decisions that caused me to self-destruct.

Many women who have absent fathers, or who have been abused and hurt, are looking for love and protection. They don't know what *true love* is, but they long to be accepted and acknowledged. We all have a God-shaped hole in our being that can only be filled by his love. When we don't know the Lord, we try to fill that hole with what we think is love.

The spirit of rejection and shame will lead us on the path of promiscuity, abortion, addiction, and other forms of destruction. Sadly, far too many men take advantage of broken, hurting women. Many broken women also take advantage of vulnerable men. True love, respect, honor, and acceptance are found only in Jesus Christ.

§

Questions to Ponder

Can you think of hurts in your past or times you felt unloved or ashamed? Have you forgiven those involved, including yourself?

How can you feel loved and worthy now that you better understand your past and God's love for you?

Perhaps you've had an abortion and are living with the regret and shame of that decision. If so, do you desire healing and to walk in the destiny God created you for?

We have all done things that caused us to live with shame, sorrow, and regret, and have harmed different areas of our lives.

The Lord does not want us to live in those places of guilt and condemnation. He wants us to repent so we can receive forgiveness and abundance and live in it. (In Chapter 5, we will go into steps of healing from abortion.[3])

In Isaiah 61, the Lord says he came to comfort the brokenhearted and to proclaim that those who have been held captive are now free. He tells those who mourn that his favor has come for them, and with it he will give a crown of beauty for their ashes. They will receive a joyful blessing instead of mourning and festive praise rather than despair. In their righteousness, they will be like great oaks that the Lord has planted for his own glory.

Did you hear that? You are the glory of God. You shine, and the Lord is pleased with you.

God loves you so much, and he desires joy and freedom for you. He wants to pick you up from this life of sorrow and despair and put you on the amazing journey he created for you.

Second Corinthians 5:17–18 says, "Anyone who belongs to Christ has become a new person. The old life is gone; a new life has begun! And all of this is a gift from God, who brought us back to himself through Christ" (NLT).

I hear the Lord calling you to come to him and sit on his lap of grace. He wants you to receive all the benefits and blessings that he paid such a high price for on the cross. He welcomes you to trade your sorrows and shame for his love and kindness. It is the greatest exchange ever. You give him your trash, and he gives you his riches and glory. You can't lose, my precious friend. Open your arms to the treasures he has for you. I invite you to pray the prayer below.

If you already know him but need freedom from hurts or decisions in your past, I urge you to sit on his lap and give him

---

[3]   Seek more in-depth healing at Pregnancy Care Centers through www. care-net.org.

your cares. Ask him to heal and restore those broken places. Let him sing you a love song of freedom.

§

Prayer

Oh, my sweet Savior Jesus, I come to you in my brokenness and pain. I ask you to forgive me for my wrong choices and all my sins.

I thank you, Father, for loving me and for sending your Son Jesus to die for me on the cross.

Lord, I ask you to wash me clean and draw close to me. I surrender my life to you, knowing that you love me and will make me new. Thank you, Lord, for destroying every stronghold and lie I have believed of the enemy. I declare every spirit of shame, rejection, and unworthiness is broken off my life. I break every agreement I made with a spirit of death in my life, and I speak your spirit of life and abundant blessing over me now.

Lord, I apply the precious blood of Jesus Christ over myself and my family line. Every spirit of the enemy must pass over and not come near my dwelling place. Lord, I thank you that you have bought my life and I am yours. I am an overcomer. I am victorious in Christ Jesus. I am the healed of the Lord. I am all that the Word of God says I am, and I have all that the Word says I have. I am seated with you in heavenly places, walking in victory in every area of my life. In Jesus' name, amen.

3. Redeemed

*"For your Maker is your husband—the L*ORD *Almighty is his name—the Holy One of Israel is your Redeemer; he is called the God of all the earth." (Isaiah 54:5)*

When you're in a deep pit, it's hard to see the light or know which way is out. You need someone to throw you a rope. Likewise, when you're drowning, you need someone to jump in to save you or throw you a lifeline.

My family had no idea about the life I was living. They knew I was troubled and things weren't good, but they didn't know about the pregnancies, abortions, drugs, or how much I was drinking. I kept it my deep, dark secret.

While Mom was in the hospital, she met a woman who knew and loved Jesus. Mom befriended her and eventually gave her life to Christ. She began her walk with the Lord after I moved out of the house, so I didn't witness her transformation. Her prayers and the nudging of the Holy Spirit brought my dad into a relationship with the Lord as well.

Many times Mom called and told me about Jesus. She shared the wonderful things he was doing in Dad's and her life. I was happy for them but was certain God wanted nothing to do with me. She told me how much Jesus loved me. *Mom doesn't know the things I've done*, I thought. *If she did, she wouldn't say that. I had three abortions, and surely a mother killing her own children is the unforgivable sin.*

Mom invited me to an event with a visiting woman evangelist. I wondered how I could get out of it. She again told me Jesus loved me, but this time it was different. She said, "Luana, I love you so much. I can't imagine a single thing you could do that would cause me not to love you. You could kill someone and I'd still love you. How much more does God love you? He created you and knows everything you've done, and he still loves you more than I ever could."

That sent a glimmer of light into my pit. Could God really love me? Would he forgive me for killing my children and all the terrible things I did? Could this be true? I thought a moment about the lifesaver she just threw me. Was I going to grab hold or let a possible opportunity go by?

It was only an hour drive, so what did I have to lose? If nothing else, I could see Mom and my sister Linda, and I wouldn't sit home alone dwelling on all my troubles.

Jesus Drops a Lifeline

When we arrived at the meeting, I sensed the enthusiasm and electricity in the room. The joy and excitement there stirred a hope in me. I didn't know what to expect, but I was ready to receive whatever I could.

Vicki Jamison preached from the Word of God. During her message, she stopped and gave prophetic words to some. Others she called forward and prayed that they'd be healed, and they experienced healing right then. I had never seen anything like that before. At the end of the meeting, she asked people to come forward if they wanted to receive Jesus as their Lord and Savior.

I didn't hesitate. I jumped up from my chair and rushed to the altar. I wanted—and needed—what she talked about. Tears overflowed from my eyes, peace covered me like a blanket, and I felt God's presence with me. It wasn't just a glimmer of light in my pit anymore. Jesus had grabbed my hand and pulled me out of the hole!

The hope that got stirred up when I entered the meeting now filled me. The joy and excitement I noticed in others came over me. I went home that day a new creation—all the old had passed away. Life was going to be different. I knew the truth that God loved me and he forgave all my sins.

The new life was difficult at first because I lived away from my family and didn't know any other Christians. Managing a fast-food restaurant required a lot of hours, and I worked most Sundays. I wasn't able to attend church and learn the Scriptures and ways of the Lord as I should. I'd never read the Bible, much less studied it, so it was all unfamiliar to me as I stumbled into unknown territory.

Many temptations and old habits of the past pounded on the door of my life. The enemy had no plans of giving up that easily. I fell and then came running back to the Lord. When things seemed good once more, I wandered away on my own path. Again, I would fall but return to the Lord. Instead of making him Lord of my life, I tried to ride the fence. I needed to get off the throne and give God his rightful position.

I felt like Paul must have when he wrote in Romans 7 about wanting to do what is good but not doing it, and not wanting to do what is wrong but doing it anyway. I had to let the revelation of Romans 8:12–17 dwell in me. It says, "Therefore, dear brothers and sisters, you have no obligation to do what your sinful nature urges you to do. For if you live by its dictates, you will die. But if through the power of the Spirit you put to death the deeds of your sinful nature, you will live. For all who are led by the Spirit of God are children of God. So you have not received a spirit that makes you fearful slaves. Instead, you received God's Spirit when he adopted you as his own children. Now we call him, 'Abba, Father.' For his Spirit joins with our spirit to affirm that we are God's children. And since we are his children, we are his heirs. In fact, together with Christ we are heirs of God's glory. But if we are to share his glory, we must also share his suffering" (NLT).

Desiring to build a solid foundation on the Word of God, I read my Bible, and Mom gave me books to read. She talked and prayed with me on the phone. I longed for friends who could mentor and encourage me in the things of the Lord, but because I worked on weekends, I wasn't able to attend church and find those relationships.

My Maker Brings a Husband

One of my employees—Mary— wanted me to meet her single brother-in-law, Steve. "I just know he's the guy for you," she said. "He's kind and gentle. Good-looking too."

Without telling me, she arranged for him to place an order at the drive-through window. Determined to refrain from dating, I stuck my head out the window, said hello, then grabbed my briefcase from the front counter and walked out the door to my car. Mary later told me that my backside so impressed her brother-in-law as I left that he returned to the restaurant for a better view.

Because Steve was laid off from his job during that time, he came in often to drink coffee and read fishing magazines while I worked. I sat and talked with him during my breaks. After a short while, I was smitten with that tall, dark, and very handsome man.

A couple of months passed before we went on an official date. He wanted to make it happen earlier, but he had been taught to not ask a woman out unless he could pay. A complete gentleman the entire evening, he opened car and building doors for me. He allowed me to go first and walked beside me in a protective manner. He escorted me to the door to say goodnight and didn't even try to kiss me. I wasn't used to being treated so kindly and with such respect. For the first time, I felt valued. My heart wanted to sing.

As we grew in our relationship, I learned that Steve had committed his life to the Lord a few years prior, but he wasn't serving him because of past hurts. We confessed our painful experiences to each other. We shared our hearts' desires and made wonderful memories. And we talked about our faith in the Lord as well as our hope in him.

After two years of dating, we made plans to get married. This time I got to shop for my own wedding dress. Dad let me choose the cake and food he would cater for the reception. I wanted the same cake as before but with pink flowers and pink water in the fountain. We served hot turkey and dressing sandwiches—my favorite—made like only Dad can make them.

I had four bridesmaids and chose my sister Lisa to be my maid of honor. Their floor-length dresses were made out of a soft, pink-colored taffeta. The girls carried off-white lace parasols adorned with flowers and ribbons. Paired with the guys in their gray tuxes and pink cummerbunds, they looked fabulous.

The most captivating man I had ever seen wore a white tux with tails. It matched my dress. As I walked up the aisle and saw him standing there, my heart leapt. I couldn't help but say, "Thank you, God, for such an amazing gift." I was in awe of his goodness to me.

Our wedding took place in a beautiful church, with a pastor officiating the ceremony—not a justice of the peace. We used wispy pink material to decorate, and on every other row of pews we placed tall metal-and-glass candelabras. It created a breathtaking picture.

Steve's mom made the flower arrangements for the church, as well as the girls' bouquets and the guys' boutonnieres. She used different shades of pink roses and white carnations with sprays of baby's breath. Two of my co-workers sang and played the piano during the ceremony. We had the reception at a friend's banquet hall. All of those details, including the weather, combined for a delightful—and special—July day.

Of course, as with any wedding, there were a few hiccups. Dad forgot some of the plates that went to the cake. That meant we had to get creative. We made them out of cardboard and hoped the cake wouldn't fall. The DJ didn't show up, so we scrambled to find a replacement as our guests filled the reception hall. What we thought were big problems at the time have now become fun memories.

Another Secret

One dark cloud hung over the day, though—something that caused me to have flashbacks of a troubled time in my life. That morning, my single, 19-year-old sister confided in me as we sat on the bed. "I'm pregnant," she said. My heart broke for her. How well I knew the pain caused from carrying a secret like that.

"I needed to tell someone," she said between sobs. "I thought you'd understand." I wrapped my arms around her and held her tight, wanting to make it all better. My tears mingled with hers.

"Does your boyfriend know?" I asked.

"Yes, but we haven't made any decisions."

As we cried together, I encouraged her to understand that her circumstances weren't hopeless and her life wasn't over.

"Promise me you won't tell anyone?" I nodded my yes.

We wiped our tears and put on happy faces to start the day's festivities, but inside I was torn apart and concerned for her future.

I held myself together until the reception came to an end, and I went into the restroom. It was my first quiet moment alone since my sister and I had talked. Tears flowed freely as I thought of the pain she would experience. I pleaded with God to direct her. "Please, Lord, don't let her go down the same destructive path I took."

Mom walked through the door just then, saw my streaked face, and immediately embraced me, concerned. "Are you okay?" she asked. "You're not regretting your decision to get married, are you?"

I assured her all was well with Steve and me, but she continued to prod. I couldn't keep the secret any longer. Mom would eventually find out, so I broke my promise to my sister and told her. We held each other and sobbed in the restroom, praying God would show up in that situation.

My sister had a miscarriage the day before her wedding several months later. She was still in the hospital, so she married her fiancé in the chapel there while sitting in a wheelchair. She wasn't able to attend her own reception, but her new husband made a quick appearance and then returned to the hospital to join her for the rest of their wedding day.

I had the privilege of helping her put on her wedding dress and prepare for the ceremony. In all the busyness of getting ready, John's mom, Ann, popped her head through the door of the hospital room. She said hello and reminded me that she still loved me.

When my sister miscarried, Mom was at the hospital to comfort her during her delivery. The Lord showed her how important it was to be there. They were allowed to hold the baby boy, touch his little fingers and toes, and say good-bye.

Mom later came to me in tears, asking forgiveness for her absence when I lost Mary. She realized that I was even younger than my sister and must have felt scared, alone, and rejected. She regretted not understanding the significance of her presence. I forgave her, and we cried together as we talked about the day of her first grandchild's birth.

God is an amazing God of healing and redemption. He says in Joel 2:19, 25, "I am sending you grain, new wine and olive oil, enough to satisfy you fully; never again will I make you an object of scorn to the nations. . . . I will repay you for the years the locusts have eaten." David, the writer of Psalm 23:3, said,

"He restores my soul. He leads me in paths of righteousness for his name's sake" (ESV).

Yes, God is faithful and always redeems the things that were stolen. Here's what Job 8:5–7 says: "But if you pray to God and seek the favor of the Almighty, and if you are pure and live with integrity, he will surely rise up and restore your happy home. And though you started with little, you will end with much" (NLT). It's an amazing promise worth claiming and declaring over your life.

Redeemed and New Beginnings

Steve and I bought a house located in an addition with three lakes, and God was fulfilling our dreams. The only thing missing was the white picket fence. I had the same job, though, which required me to work most Sundays. Steve stayed involved in fishing, hunting, bowling, and other activities that kept him from church as well.

Months after our nuptials we started to experience trouble. I thought marriage meant doing life together. I wanted companionship and a close, loving relationship. Steve wanted to do the things he did before, and fit me in when he could. It wasn't working so well. We fought a lot.

I called Mom during that time. She had grown in the Lord and developed into a mighty prayer warrior. Mom participated in several prayer groups and Bible studies, and her wisdom and counsel were an immense help. She prayed with me and said, "You need to go to a Word church, even if it means finding a new job and going by yourself." She gave me a book called *Prayers That Avail Much*. It was a book of prayers formed from Scriptures, and it became my lifeline as I prayed God's Word for Steve and our marriage.

Late one Saturday night, as I drove home from work, I saw a bright light shining down on the building ahead. The little gray structure glowed, and I quickly pulled into the gravel parking lot to look at the sign in front. It read Milan Foursquare Church. That puzzled me. I had driven that road, past that church, hundreds of times on my way to and from work and never saw it.

God illuminated it that night. He was leading me by his Holy Spirit once again to bring me life. I rifled through my car to find a piece of paper and wrote down the service times, promising the Lord I would be there in the morning.

Clearly, God showed me that he was answering my prayers. He is my maker and my husband. He is my redeemer and first love. He gave me Steve as my helpmate, but God wanted me to make him my first and greatest love so that he could put all things in right order.

Matthew 6:33 serves as a great reminder of that. "Seek the Kingdom of God above all else, and live righteously, and he will give you everything you need" (NLT).

This was my promise to the Lord that night: "I will serve you above everything else, Lord, and trust you to care for me no matter what happens."

I went to church the next morning by myself. The building was small and run-down, but the people inside were alive and filled with the love of Jesus. Many introduced themselves and asked questions. They were genuinely interested in getting to know me. The warmth and love they had made me feel at home immediately. I couldn't get enough, and in the days ahead I was there whenever the doors were opened.

Steve saw a change in my attitude. He noticed the joy and excitement I had about the Lord. His curiosity caused him to come with me one Sunday, and it wasn't long before both of us were sold out to the Lord and wanted all he had in store for us. We became a part of that little family. We learned to study the Word, pray more effectively, and love unselfishly. We filled leadership positions in the church. We formed friendships with people and allowed their wisdom and love to splash over us and shape us into vessels of honor for the Lord.

Steve and I experienced the Lord perform wonderful miracles in our lives. I had been diagnosed with Bell's palsy about a year before we were married, and the Lord completely healed me. I have no symptoms to this day. I also smoked cigarettes. I hated that habit and knew I was polluting the precious temple God gave me. It was bondage. In the middle of church services and meetings, I yearned to smoke. Because I was ashamed, I hid my cigarettes.

One weekend, I attended a conference with Mom and Linda, and the speaker invited people who wanted prayer to come forward. I went as fast as I could. She stood in front of me and asked about my needs. "I want to be free of the addiction of cigarettes," I said. She spoke a simple prayer and went to the next person.

The desire didn't leave, so I remained standing there. After she prayed with all the others, she returned to me and asked if I had another need. I told her, "I don't want to crave or desire a cigarette anymore." She instructed me to go and remove the cigarettes from my purse.

When I got back to her, she had me close my eyes. "Throw the cigarettes across the room and imagine that you're throwing them into a stream of the blood of Jesus. Once they're under his blood, you can't reach in to retrieve them." I did as she said. Immediately the desire left and I was delivered from the addiction of nicotine. I never smoked another cigarette.

About a year into our marriage, the economy bottomed out and Steve got laid off again from his job. The Lord provided work for both of us. We didn't make as much pay as Steve's original position, but we watched as God miraculously met all our needs. We wrote the tithe check first and then paid our bills. Our checkbook always balanced when many times the numbers didn't add up.

Life was difficult but never more rewarding. Steve and I were happy. We learned to trust the Lord in those difficult times.

§

Thoughts to Ponder

Some of you reading this may feel as if you're not worthy to be forgiven, that your sin is too great and is beyond God's love. I want to assure you that nothing you can ever do is beyond God's love for you.

Here's what Paul wrote in Romans 8:38–39: "I am convinced that nothing can ever separate us from God's love. Neither death nor life, neither angels nor demons, neither ours fears for today nor our worries about tomorrow—not even the powers of hell can separate us from God's love. No power in the sky above or in the earth below—indeed, nothing in all creation will ever be able to separate us from the love of God that is revealed in Christ Jesus our Lord" (NLT).

Let that powerful promise sink in for a minute. God is always for you. He created you. He wants the best for you. If bad things happen in your life, they don't come from God—they're from the enemy. God isn't waiting for you to do something wrong or for you to mess up so he can pound on you and punish you. He created you with a plan and purpose.

Galatians 1:15 says, "But even before I was born, God chose me and called me by his marvelous grace" (NLT).

His Word says in Psalm 139 that he knit you together in your mother's womb. He laid out every moment of your life even before you lived one single day. His thoughts about you are precious and plentiful. In fact, God has so many thoughts about you that they can't be numbered or counted. He says they outnumber the grains of sand. Imagine that. When you wake up, he is still right there with you.

Does that sound like someone who doesn't care about you or love you? For far too long we have believed the lies of the enemy that God is out to get us. It is just not true.

Jesus died for us when we were still in our sin. Actually, our sin is WHY he did it. God wants to be with us and have relationship with us so badly that he gave up his one and only Son, Jesus. Think about this: The Son of God left heaven to come to earth and die for us, for no other reason than that we could live with him forever. It's a picture of true love, and it absolutely blows my mind. There is no greater love than to lay down your life for someone. Jesus took our sins upon himself so we wouldn't have to face the punishment of being separated from God for eternity.

Let God's Holy Spirit breathe that amazing truth over you. Take hold of the beautiful gift of forgiveness, salvation, and eternal life God has already purchased and given to you.

If you want the wonderful gift God has set before you, let's untie the ribbon and remove the wrap together—let's open the miraculous, victorious life God spoke over and wrote specifically for you. It's yours. You just need to receive it. Please join me in praying the prayer below.

§

Prayer

Lord, I thank you for the price you paid for my life. I ask that you forgive me for the times I have sinned by choosing my own selfish ways. I receive your free gift of love, forgiveness, and salvation. I surrender to your plans and purposes for my life and know they are good because you love me. Thank you for saving me and setting me free from the guilt, shame, and lies of my past. Lord, I ask you to baptize me in your perfect love and help me to embrace it. Amen.

§

Now, Lord, I pray over these precious ones that you have called by name from darkness into your marvelous light and love. I declare that the lies of the enemy over their lives are broken in Jesus' name. Lord, you have written each one of their books, so I say to the enemy, "IT IS WRITTEN that these dear individuals are more than overcomers in Christ Jesus, and their names are written on the palm of God's hand. You have no power or authority over their lives." I thank you, Jesus, for guarding and protecting their destinies. Hide them in your secret place and reveal your mysteries to them. In Jesus' name, amen.

4. The Song

"Sing, barren woman, you who never bore a child; burst into song, shout for joy, you who were never in labor; because more are the children of the desolate woman than of her who has a husband." (Isaiah 54:1)

God was so good to us, and we loved watching him work in our lives. After we had been married a while, we asked God if it was his desire and time for us to start a family. Steve and I were excited at the thought of becoming parents. Because of my previous pregnancies—some that happened even while on birth control—I was certain news of a little one would come quickly.

As months passed without my conceiving, concern took over. I had no troubles getting pregnant in the past, so Steve went for a checkup. The doctor found an issue and took care of it with a minor surgery. Within a few weeks Steve healed, everything looked okay, and we were off to the baby races again.

We still had no success. That meant it was my turn to get checked out, which evolved into what seemed like never-ending tests. I felt like a human pincushion on display for all to see. It was an exhaustive, difficult time, but Steve and I grew closer and hung on to God's Word.

All my examinations sent me to one clinic after another, with my feet up in stirrups again and again. During each appointment I had flashbacks of the abortion facilities and the horror and pain that came with it—a constant reminder of my sin and the killing of my children. I wondered if the Lord was punishing me. He had given me four beautiful gifts of life, and I spit in his face. Now I welcomed and so desperately wanted a child, but he wasn't answering my cry. I wasn't blaming him—I just figured I didn't deserve a baby. Every appointment got harder, and I struggled with forgiving myself.

With multiple tests, including some at The University of Iowa Hospital, the medical professionals couldn't find the problem. My OB-GYN doctor then scheduled a dye test, which involves running dye through the uterus and tubes to look for blockages and problems. I hadn't told any of the doctors about my abortions because I was still too ashamed. Of course I told Steve before we got married, though, because he deserved to know my past before committing to our future. He was accepting and loving of my confession and didn't judge me.

Sing, O Barren Woman

The doctor watched the screen as the injected dye flowed into my uterus and tubes. "Have you ever had an abortion?" she asked. I couldn't lie, so I admitted to having three.

She turned the screen toward me and pointed out places she saw damage and blockages. "Do you see this? One of your tubes is 90% blocked. The other one here is 100% blocked." Her voice was gentle as she said, "You will never get pregnant. The abortion procedures caused so much damage to your tubes and uterus that you're infertile.

"If you keep trying to have children, you could have an ectopic pregnancy. And that could be fatal." As she removed her gloves and washed her hands, she told me about the risks and dangers involved with an ectopic pregnancy. "Call my office in the next few days, and let's get a hysterectomy scheduled soon." She walked to the exam table, patted my knee, and told me I could get dressed. Then she and her assistant stepped out the door, leaving me alone with my thoughts.

It seemed as though the air had been sucked out of the room. I gasped in an effort to breathe, but sobs of regret and repentance for what I had done is what came out. I couldn't move my body. I just wanted to stay on the exam table, curl up into a ball, and cry. Questions raced through my mind. What just happened? How was I going to tell Steve this news? How do I tell my husband that he will never be a father and it's my fault?

The reality started to sink in. *I killed the only children I would ever bear.* I would never feel the kick of a child in my womb. I would never experience my abdomen growing large and my husband placing his hand on it to feel the movement of our baby. I would never be in the delivery room with Steve, anticipating the arrival of our first bundle of joy.

What did I do by making those choices years prior, not just to myself but to my husband and family as well? The consequences of those sins were stealing more of my life and my husband's dreams, and possibly destroying my marriage.

I lay there and prayed once again for God to forgive me for the abortions. "Lord, please give me courage and strength to tell Steve. Walk with us through this trial. We can't do it without you." Just then, the words in Philippians 4:13 came to mind. "I can do all things through Christ who strengthens me" (NKJV). I was able to get up from the table and get dressed.

I returned home and gave Steve the report. His response was kind and selfless. As much as the news hurt him, he was even more concerned for my pain. We held each other and cried, grieving the loss of the family we dreamt about. We prayed for God's plan to unfold and to show us his will.

God's grace over us and the compassion of my husband awed me. I was fearful of how Steve would react to the information, wondering if he'd want a divorce. I knew how it felt to be rejected and thrown away, but the way he treated me was different. Steve truly honored, cherished, and loved me because he had the love of the Father. His commitment and character were an example of Jesus' faithfulness. In that moment, God gave me assurance that he would work this out for our good. It may not look like what we had expected, but in the end God would get the glory.

Burst into Song and Shout for Joy

You may have places in your life where things didn't turn out the way you had desired. Dreams disappear and hopes get dashed, but God is the source of hope, and he's the one who planted those dreams in you. Never give up, dear one, for the Lord never gives up on you.

Isaiah 55:8–13 says, "My thoughts are nothing like your thoughts," says the LORD. "And my ways are far beyond anything you could imagine. For just as the heavens are higher than the earth, so my ways are higher than your ways and my thoughts higher than your thoughts.

"The rain and snow come down from the heavens and stay on the ground to water the earth. They cause the grain to grow, producing seed for the farmer and bread for the hungry. It is the same with my word. I send it out, and it always produces fruit. It will accomplish all I want it to, and it will prosper everywhere I send it.

"You will live in joy and peace. The mountains and hills will burst into song, and the trees of the field will clap their hands! Where once there were thorns, cypress trees will grow. Where nettles grew, myrtles will sprout up. These events will bring great honor to the LORD's name; they will be an everlasting sign of his power and love" (NLT).

God is always for you. He is always working for your good and his glory. Many times when things aren't going as we planned, or we have disappointments in our life, we allow the enemy to beat us or bring discouragement. God purposes to turn those situations into opportunities to build character in you and for you to trust in him. I've heard it said that you can't have a message unless you have a mess; you can't have a testimony unless you have a test. Faith in God grows from the places we depended on him, not from the times we did things on our own.

A wonderful promise to stand on when we face disappointments or opposition is found in Deuteronomy 31:6. "So be strong and courageous! Do not be afraid and do not panic before them. For the LORD your God will personally go ahead of you. He will neither fail you nor abandon you" (NLT).

The Lord says you will never have to do it alone. He is personally going with you. I can't imagine facing life's trials without him.

In Hebrews 13:5–6, the Lord assures us again. "I will never fail you. I will never abandon you." So we can say with confidence, "The LORD is my helper, so I will have no fear. What can mere people do to me?" (NLT). I recommend that you get this promise engrained in you. Trust him in everything, because he is trustworthy.

§

Things to Ponder

I encourage you to look back on the path of your life. Do you see the places the Lord carried you when you didn't have the means to walk anymore?

When times are hard and discouraging, we need to take a position of dance and sing a song of thankfulness. Our God has been good to us and will continue to be good to us. As we sing, joy comes into our wilderness—peace and hope sprout. Those dead, dry places will see opportunities and life if we water them with gratitude. We will be able to soar to a place where we see God's steadfastness and we can trust him with the outcomes.

In Isaiah 43:18–19, God promises his faithfulness. "But forget all that—it is nothing compared to what I am going to do. For I am about to do something new. See, I have already begun! Do you not see it? I will make a pathway through the wilderness. I will create rivers in the dry wasteland" (NLT).

Can you begin to thank God for the blessings in your life and ask him to reveal himself in the difficult places?

Praise Jesus in hard times

Move the furniture to the sides of the room so you have lots of space. Put on some praise music and begin to dance and worship your Lord. Listen intently, focusing only on him as you dance and move. Holy Spirit will come and shift your attitude and outlook, and you will be in a position of peace as you go through your hard times.

Take heart in these words from Zephaniah 3:17. "For the LORD your God is living among you. He is a mighty savior. He will take delight in you with gladness. With his love, he will calm all your fears. He will rejoice over you with joyful songs."

§

Prayer

Lord, I hear you singing over those reading this now. You are serenading them with a song written uniquely for them. You delight in them. I pray you will flood these dear people with your peace and bring assurance of your love. Let them hear your melodious words so they will know how much you treasure them. Fill them with faith so they can stand on your Word and your promises. Help them sing with you through the sorrows and wilderness times of their lives. Amen.

5. Forgiveness Received

*"So now I have sworn not to be angry with you, never to
rebuke you again. Though the mountains be shaken and the
hills be removed, yet my unfailing love for you will not be
shaken nor my covenant of peace be removed," says the LORD,
who has compassion on you. (Isaiah 54:9–10)*

Steve and I prayed for God's will. What was his heart for
us? Did he want us to have children? Were we to adopt,
become foster parents, have in vitro fertilization, or was he
going to heal my body? We stood on God's Word of healing
for my body. We waited, listened, and kept busy working for
the kingdom of God.

A Governmental Calling

I had the privilege of helping my friend Pat Herath on a
presidential campaign for Pat Robertson. We love our country
and desired a godly leader to restore our nation back to righteousness and the fear of the Lord.

Together we traveled to numerous cities making phone calls
and knocking on doors. We planned events for Pat Robertson so
people could meet him and hear his plan for our nation. Many

of the wonderful people we met became lifelong friends. We also learned about our country's political process.

At one point Pat was working on an entire day of campaign stops for Pat Robertson. It took a lot of planning, phone calling, and hard work to set up all those events. The day before, Pat and I drove to the city where the first gathering would take place. She had her orange Volkswagen van loaded to the top with everything we needed for the day.

Snow started falling and didn't let up. We walked the frozen white streets, praying for our nation and for God to stop the snow. It wasn't safe for anyone to be out in that weather, especially for Pat, as he was coming from a distance. When we went to bed, we didn't know what the next day would bring.

I had a dream that night—we saw Pat Robertson in a Hardee's restaurant. It was crowded with people, and he greeted each one. When I awakened, my friend Pat was on the phone and looked concerned as she listened. She hung up and tearfully said, "Pat Robertson won't be at the first stop. They don't know if he will be able to make any of the events today."

The news distressed her, so we prayed for God to intervene and for everyone's safety. Afterward, I told Pat about my dream. She screamed with joy, grabbed the agenda from her bag of papers and binders, and showed me the itinerary for the day. The third stop was scheduled at a Hardee's restaurant. We laughed and thanked God for the revelation. He gave us confirmation that Pat Robertson would be at the third stop, and sure enough he was.

We had wonderful God moments and opportunities while we volunteered on the campaign. For the first time, we attended a national convention and experienced the procedure of delegates electing a nominee. That began my involvement in our nation's political processes at the national and state level. It birthed a love in me for the government our founders established—a government that gives freedom, one that is for the people and by the people. I am grateful to the Lord and Pat for that season in my life.

At the time the campaign ended, I still had not conceived. Steve and I continued to believe and wait on God's plans. Our desire for a child grew stronger, so we researched our options in greater depth. If we adopted or became foster parents, we would need a home study done. We would also need to take classes through the state. We enrolled in the classes and began the next step.

His Unfailing Love Will Not Be Shaken

During that process, the Lord took me through a very personal journey of healing. Steve worked third shift, so I was alone every night. God allowed me to mourn the loss of my children. I cried for what I did and for what I lost. I grieved over who they were supposed to be and what they were called to do. What did they look like? What was the color of their hair and eyes? Were they girls or boys? What were their names? What was missing in our lives?

I had missed first steps, first words, first dates, birthdays, proms, graduations, and weddings. And then it hit me that I would miss out on future grandchildren. That didn't just affect me; it changed my family tree. Members of my family were missing—grandchildren, great grandchildren, and many generations to come.

The more I pondered and mourned those things, the more the enemy came and condemned me for all I had done. Again I went down the path of thinking that maybe I couldn't have kids because God was angry and punishing me for the sins I committed. I didn't deserve children after killing the ones he tried to give me. Those thoughts tormented me greatly. I spent hours crying and asking God to forgive me. I related to the story of Jacob in the Bible when he wrestled with God for his blessing, but I wasn't sure who I was wrestling with. Was it me, the enemy, or God? Did I deserve a blessing?

On the nights Steve was home, he held me as I cried. He tried to convince me of his love for me and that he had forgiven me for the decisions I made in my past. I beat myself up because Steve wasn't a part of my life when I committed those sins, yet he had to live with the consequences of them. I felt guilty and responsible for his pain.

I questioned if God really forgave me for the abortions. Maybe he pardoned the rest of my sins, but killing three children was too much. It crossed the line. And then, if God forgave me, could I forgive myself? I struggled with believing that his grace was that expansive.

As my thoughts taunted me, I knew the enemy could take me down a hopeless route if I didn't grab hold of the Lord. I chose to go on that wilderness journey with the One who pulled me out before. I sat with my open Bible, a pen and journal, and a box of tissues. When the enemy pulled on my mind, I asked the Lord to bring me truth. It was the hardest road but also the best road. The Lord spoke to me in amazing ways.

God revealed to me that the places we'd go would be dark, but he was with me. He wasn't angry and wouldn't condemn me or dwell on my sins. He wanted me to go back so he could bring healing and wholeness to those old wounds and areas of brokenness once and for all. The words in the verse at the beginning of this chapter rang true for me. Though my mountains be shaken and my hills be removed, his unfailing love for me would not be shaken.

Breaking Soul Ties

God first dealt with the sexual relationships in my past. Intercourse spiritually binds two people together, and the Bible considers them married. The two become one flesh. I gave a piece of myself to each person I had sex with, just as they gave a piece of themselves to me. This is called a soul tie.

The Lord taught me to sever and renounce the ties with those men through prayer. I asked God to forgive me for each sexual relationship I had out of wedlock. I prayed to destroy my bonds with each man. I called back the fragments of myself I gave away and released the fragments of the men back to each of them. I spiritually saw those fragments and remnants return. Cracks and broken places filled in and were healed. Ambitions and aspirations I had forgotten returned. God was making me whole again. He was at work restoring me to who he created me to be.

The Process of Forgiveness and Healing

In my mind, God took me to the abortion facility. I saw the doctor and nurses and those involved, and God asked me to forgive them. Mentally I went to each one individually and told them I forgave them for deceiving me and for the part they played in my abortions. I saw the face of each boyfriend who participated in that selfish scheme as an accomplice. I wrote letters, telling them about Jesus and asking them to forgive me for my part. I asked Steve's permission to do that because I didn't want to dishonor or disrespect him.

The Lord also showed me how I had changed my family tree. He asked me to go to my parents and siblings and seek forgiveness for removing members from our family. I needed prayer because I didn't want to give the enemy any place, or hurt and offend those I loved.

No one in my family knew I had abortions except Linda. She had a relationship with the Lord and prayed with me many times. I'm sure her prayers years ago were instrumental in bringing me into the kingdom of God. I called Linda, and we prayed on the phone together. Later, I contacted each family member and asked if they could meet at our parents' house so Steve and I could talk to them.

That night Linda, her husband, Roger, and Steve and I walked around my parents' house seven times, praying for the presence of the Lord to come and move in all their hearts and minds. God showed me beforehand that the enemy was trying to build walls of offense and accusation like in Jericho[4], and if we walked and prayed, those walls would come down. It had to be quite a sight to see the four of us marching around my parents' house seven times—from front to back in the dark, through bushes, and all while praying loudly and commanding the enemy to flee.

After we finished, we came in through the back door. Everyone had arrived, and they were seated around the dining room table. When I first glanced in and saw my siblings and parents there, I had flashbacks of the night John and I told Mom and Dad we were pregnant. I had the same pit in my stomach, but it wasn't because of fear and shame. God was with me this time, and even though I was confessing my sin, the guilt and shame had no hold on me. God's covenant of peace couldn't be removed. I was there to ask forgiveness and bring restoration to my family.

At first we exchanged pleasantries and small talk, and then I shared about my past. By the time I got to the abortions, I was crying and couldn't finish. Steve filled in until I pulled myself together. I looked at my siblings one by one and asked, "Will you forgive me for taking the lives of your nieces and nephews? You'll never get to know them or teach them your crazy antics because of me."

Before facing my parents, I stopped to wipe my eyes. "Mom . . . Dad . . . will you forgive me for killing your three grandbabies?" I hesitated for a few seconds to gather my emotions. "You'll

---

[4]   See Joshua 6 for the story about the walls of Jericho.

never get to hold them or spoil them or brag about them to your friends. My selfish choices ruined that for you."

I admitted my remorse for changing our family dynamics. If those three babies had lived, circumstances would be different. Every Christmas and holiday would be a little more crowded. We'd have more birthday celebrations and fun-filled family outings. I had stolen the delightful moments my parents would have enjoyed with grandchildren. I stopped laughter and conversations from passing through the atmosphere. Each of their lives would have touched and added to ours in special ways that now would not happen.

My own plans replaced God's plans, and I robbed the glory he would have received through those precious little ones. I didn't take that lightly. Life is holy to God, and I will never know all the repercussions of my sins.

My family showed love and compassion—something I didn't expect. Both Mom and Dad got up from their chairs and held me tight, saying they forgave me. Each of my siblings also expressed their forgiveness. As we left that night, I couldn't help but raise my head to the sky and whisper words of thanks to my wonderful Father. The secret I feared—and that haunted me for so long—was now a weapon in my hand against the enemy and being used for unity and love in my family.

Seeing My Children

The Lord gave me another amazing gift—the opportunity to see my children. He asked me one day if I wanted to know their genders and names. "You know I do, Lord," I said, and as I closed my eyes, I saw four beautiful siblings running and playing on a playground. They were so happy and full of life as they interacted with other kids. God allowed me to view the expressions on their faces and the color of their eyes and hair. I observed their little personalities and talents.

As I looked at each one, a name came into my heart. I called out that name, and the child stopped, glanced over, and ran to me, yelling "Mommy! Mommy!" Soon I had four beautiful children wrapped around me in a group hug. They kissed me and jumped on me and asked me to play.

My gracious Lord even let me see Mary, the daughter I miscarried. The others were Ashley, Ruth, and Joseph. Three girls and a boy piled on top of me. We held hands and sang. We played tag and hide-and-seek. We sat in the lush green grass picking wild flowers and making necklaces out of them. The kids and I laughed as I tickled them and spun them around. They didn't hate me, nor were they angry with me.

I feared when I got to heaven that my children wouldn't want anything to do with me for taking their lives. I didn't know how I'd explain why I killed them. Those fears were put to rest as we played together. I experienced their unconditional love. No blame. No bitterness. Not even a question of why. Just peace, joy, and love. What a precious blessing the Lord gave me! I felt the gaping holes in me fill with his unfailing love.

He walked me through grieving the loss of my sweet children and allowed me to see his watchcare over them. God assured me that I would get to spend time with them soon. My mourning turned to singing and dancing. Yes, I still regret the choices I made to take their lives, but I have peace knowing I am forgiven and will see them again.

Sharing My Secrets

The Lord tugged on my heart to share my secret of abortion with others. My friend Pat served on the steering committee to start a Pregnancy Resource Center in our area and asked me to help with some of her assigned duties. She didn't know I had abortions in my past.

After attending a Christian concert one night, I asked Pat if we could talk. We sat in the theater seats, and I cautiously told her about my hidden history. With complete love and acceptance, Pat graciously listened and prayed with me. More chains fell off, and greater freedom filled my heart. She suggested I discuss my past with my pastor, sensing it would bring even more healing.

Every step of the journey pushed me to face my fears. And whenever I took a step trusting the Lord, he slew another giant. The accusing army got smaller and smaller. Each time I confessed my former sins without condemnation, I felt release and more empowered to share again.

I took Pat's advice and set up a meeting with Pastor Rick and his wife, Beth. We sat around a table in a Sunday school room at church, and I talked about the abortions and the effect they had on me physically, spiritually, and psychologically. Again, I was met with love and compassion.

Pastor Rick encouraged me to recount my story to others so they could know the devastation of abortion. "Would you be willing to talk about it at church?" he asked. I was reluctant but knew it was God's strategy. The Lord wants us to understand the consequences of sin. He also wants us to know his forgiveness and freedom.

I gave my testimony during a church service, and the Lord used it to bring restoration for others and myself. He also opened the door for more speaking opportunities.

Learning More of the Deception of Abortion

Pat was learning how to organize banquets for our local Pregnancy Resource Center, so she invited Steve and me to attend an event at another pregnancy center. The speaker that night was Carol Everett, author of the book *Blood Money*. Carol had owned several abortion facilities in Texas and had an abortion herself. After one of her employees led her to the Lord, she realized that abortion takes innocent lives. She closed her clinics and started a pro-life ministry, speaking the truth of what happens behind the doors.

I went through many emotions as Carol spoke. She talked about abortion being a multi- billion-dollar industry and how she purchased her first center from just one month's abortion sales. The number of abortions performed determined the abortionists' earnings. Because they received cash, no 1099s or W-2s were needed.

Carol had the goal of becoming a millionaire. Rather than providing healthcare, her line of work was about the profit to be made; therefore, her facilities had a hefty marketing budget. I tried to get my head wrapped around the idea of advertising the killing of innocent children to their mothers. Somehow that seemed terribly wrong. But more abortions meant more money. The women were a number and a dollar amount.

"The abortion industry has a plan to sell abortions. It's called sex education," she said. "First, we went into the schools to break down kids' natural modesty. The purpose was to sepa-rate them from their parents and their values so we became the sex experts in their lives. We then invited them to the clinics to get reduced-cost birth control pills and condoms to pro-mote sexual activity. When the kids came to the clinics, we gave them very low-dose birth control pills or defective con-doms. We didn't buy the most expensive ones—we bought the cheapest. That way when the birth control failed and they got pregnant, they would call the 'experts,' and we'd be guaran-teed repeat business. We could sell them an abortion and more birth control pills."

Here's the bottom line: that plan causes a vicious, hopeless cycle for the women, but it also generates financial security and lots of profits for the abortion providers.

Marketing Abortions

Carol further explained how their scheme worked. "The staff members who answered phones are called counselors. But really they're just telemarketers, because abortion is a skillfully-marketed product sold to a very frightened person in crisis. We would say things like, 'Is this good news or bad news?' And we knew full well it was bad news if they were calling for an abortion. Then we would say, 'We can take care of your problem and no one needs to know.' The sales people were trained to identify the girls' fear and find out if they had any objections to abortion. If they could overcome the objection, they got the sale."

She even shared how they played on the girls' fears and vulnerabilities. They reached over, grabbed them by the bony part of their elbows, and squeezed to get their attention. Then they'd say, "If you have the money, we can take care of this right now." They knew if the girls left the clinic without an abortion, they might lose the sale. So they identified any apprehension and used it to affirm an abortion decision.

Carol also spoke about how they saved money by not sterilizing instruments. They performed twenty to thirty abortions an hour and had only twenty-one sets of instruments. At that pace, there was no time to sterilize the instruments. The regulations and laws for other medical facilities don't apply to the abortion industry, so they could get away with just about anything.

The more she talked, the sicker I became. My emotions went wild, with sadness and betrayal first. Then anger followed. So much had been taken from me because of greed. My heart hurt for the women who needed help but ended up deceived and abused instead. The lies of the abortion industry outraged me. "You can trust us," they say. "We're a healthcare provider." They pretend to care, but they kill children and destroy women—all for the almighty dollar. What they refuse to admit is that they're dealing with people's lives, not just numbers on a piece of paper.

As that revelation sunk in, I couldn't stop crying. I felt nauseous. I looked for ways to get out of the room without someone seeing me, but I didn't see any. Carol noticed me and how emotional I was. Right after she finished her talk, she came down and held me tight. She asked for forgiveness for those who hurt me so deeply.

Her talk was a watershed experience for me. It shifted my thinking. No longer was this just about my healing—it was something much bigger. God wants everyone to know the truth about the pain and devastation abortion causes. He wants women to experience his love, and he longs to set them free from the torment of that evil. Just as the Scripture at the beginning of this chapter says, God is not angry with you. His unfailing love for you is not shaken, nor is his covenant of peace removed. He has compassion for you.

If you are a woman who has been hurt by abortion, please contact Carol and her ministry for help[5].

Finding My Purpose

When I got home that night, I asked God what he wanted me to do with the new truth I learned. I heard his voice loud and clear. "Go tell anyone who will listen."

Psalm 139:13–18 and Jeremiah 29:11–12 came alive to me. God formed each of those little ones in their mothers' wombs. He had a plan and a purpose for them before they lived a single day of their lives. He says he knows the plans he has for us. They are for good and not for disaster, to give us a future and a hope.

God knew and thought about each one of those babies and moms. We can't take an innocent life because it's inconvenient

---

[5]   Carol Everett's website: www.heidigroup.org

at that time in our life. We are each made in his likeness, which means abortion destroys his creation. It's an assault on God himself.

I had a mission, and it burned within me. I now knew how much the Father had forgiven me because I knew the depth of my sin. That forgiveness came at a high price. Jesus suffered immensely and, ultimately, he died. Father God and his only Son were separated so Father God and you (or me) wouldn't have to be.

Knowing the intensity of God's plan showed me the length he would go to be with me. He truly loved me. As I heard my Father's voice, I said, "Yes, yes, yes!" It wasn't out of duty or guilt but from sheer adoration for him who valued me so much. The Lord continued to reveal that mission, and he opened doors of opportunity for me to walk through.

The Adoption Process

Steve and I sensed the Lord wanted us to adopt. We started the process and asked the state to place foster children in our home who were high risk and eligible for adoption. We cared for several kids but weren't able to adopt any of them.

A friend of Bob and Pat helped start an adoption agency in St. Louis, called Love Basket[6]. The organization did domestic and foreign adoptions. They had several places from which to adopt, but the Lord gave us a love for the people of India. With excitement we chose that country.

Foreign adoption wasn't new to our family. Linda always dreamt of having lots of children, but because of medical reasons she was unable to conceive. She and Roger adopted a son and daughter from Korea. They were a huge help to us as we went through the paperwork and other requirements of the process.

---

[6] Love Basket Adoption Agency (www.lovebasket.org)

They said it would take nine months to a year to complete everything required before we could have our adopted child in our home. That seemed reasonable, especially since pregnancies last nine months.

Soon we received a letter with a picture of a beautiful baby boy named Naveen. The agency asked us to pray and ask the Lord if Naveen was the child for us. Our hearts melted immediately, and we sensed that God had handpicked this little guy for us. We looked up the definition of Naveen. It meant "new beginnings." The name was perfect because it was a new beginning for all of us.

We prayed for the paperwork to be completed in a timely fashion and for documents to get where they needed to go without being lost. We also prayed for our new son and felt the Lord wanted to add to his name. He would become Zachary Naveen, which means "precious gift from God" and "new beginnings."

We prepared our hearts and our home for his arrival. The Lord truly was not angry with me, and the sins of my past had not shaken his unfailing love. He was compassionate and showed me that nothing I did could change the way he felt about me. He had been—and always would be—for my good. Not only did he answer our hearts' desire, he also restored the lost birthright I selfishly gave away.

Spending Time with Jesus

Perhaps as you're reading this you may have triggered memories or stirred-up emotions because of an abortion in your past. I encourage you to sit before the Lord and allow him to take you through the healing journey. It may be different from the path I took, or it may be similar. I assure you that the pain you experience in the process will be worth it. God is gentle and will take you only where you are willing to go. He promises to always accompany you and will even carry you if needed.

The Lord doesn't intend to hurt you or to rub your face in all the mistakes you've made. No, his plan is quite the contrary. Give him permission to gingerly walk with you back to those places of devastation. Let him carefully and gently wash and cleanse your infected wounds. He will wipe them with the balm of his Word so they can heal once and for all. Then he will walk you forward to your today in such forgiveness and completeness that you will no longer live from those sources of pain and brokenness. Instead, you will move ahead from a place of wholeness.

Your entire life and the lens through which you see things will change, as well as the position from which you act and react. Your perspective will now come from a place of love, compassion, and wholeness. If hurting people cause damage to others, then those who are healthy will bring well-being and vitality.

If you feel that the healing journey is too hard, or you need additional help, please know you can call any Pregnancy Resource Center. They offer abortion recovery programs and one-on-one encouragement. And they will speak to you in total confidence and love.[7]

§

Questions to Ponder

Are you waiting for the desires of your heart to be fulfilled? What are they?

Have you given away pieces of your life and heart that you wish you could get back? If so, will you walk through the steps of breaking soul ties?

---

[7] Visit www.care-net.org for a listing of Pregnancy Resource Centers in your area.

What would it take for you to believe God is not angry with you and you are worthy of his love?

What secrets are you hiding behind, fearing rejection if they were known?

We all have questions and concerns. You are not alone. I encourage you to set down this book and take a pen and paper and begin to talk to the Lord about them. Listen for his loving voice. He longs to hear from you and promises to answer. In Matthew 7:7–8 he says, "Keep on asking, and you will receive what you ask for. Keep on seeking, and you will find. Keep on knocking, and the door will be opened to you. For everyone who asks, receives. Everyone who seeks, finds. And to everyone who knocks, the door will be opened" (NLT).

Be still before the Lord and know that he cares deeply for you. Listen closely, then write down what you hear him say. You will be amazed at his love and compassion for you.

John 15:13–16 says, "Greater love has no one than this: to lay down one's life for one's friends. You are my friends if you do what I command. I no longer call you servants, because a servant does not know his master's business. Instead, I have called you friends, for everything that I learned from my Father I have made known to you. You did not choose me, but I chose you and appointed you so that you might go and bear fruit—fruit that will last—and so that whatever you ask in my name the Father will give you" (NIV).

Jesus loves you so much that he freely laid down his life for you. He calls you his friend. Ponder that for a moment and let it sink in. The creator of all the heavens and the earth—God—calls you his friend. With a friend like that, who can be harmed by an enemy?

Write on your pages all he tells you. Hide it in your heart. Let those words be the foundational stones you build your faith upon. Let those words be your fountain of life. Let this be a new habit you form with the Lord.

The more time you spend listening to him, the more you will know his voice. You will learn to believe only his voice and not that of the enemy.

Let me pray for you as you begin journaling what God wants to speak into you.

§

Prayer

Lord, you are so tender, and you long to spend time with your precious children. I ask you to open the floodgates of heaven and allow your Word to wash over these dear ones. Would you answer their questions and refute every lie the enemy has told them?

Hold them close, Lord, and take them to intimate places with you. Show them your vastness and your great love for them. Lord, I pray you show them the words you have written about their lives. Breathe life on them that sets them free. Place them on the path of healing and restoration and bring every desire of their hearts to pass, for you have planted those desires there.

Lord, please help them to grow in stature and wisdom and wholeness. Destroy every yoke of unworthiness and hopelessness from them, for they are yours and you care for them.

Now, Lord, I declare the precious blood of Jesus over them. You are their guard and protector, and they have a firm foundation that is set in the Word of God. Give them the mind of Christ and bring all their thoughts captive to that mind. I declare that their minds will be set on the things above and not on the things of this world.

Lord, I ask this all in your name—the name that is above every name--Jesus.

6. Rebuilding with Precious Stones

"Afflicted city, lashed by storms and not comforted, I will rebuild you with stones of turquoise, your foundations with lapis lazuli. I will make your battlements of rubies, your gates of sparkling jewels, and all your walls of precious stones." (Isaiah 54:11–12)

Oh, the waiting. Waiting on the things we want can be hard. Hurry and get that paperwork in. Now wait. Hurry and get those documents signed. Now wait. Finally, we had everything completed and approved—it certainly wouldn't be long now.

We waited and waited, and then the adoption agency alerted us about a problem. The Indian government had new judges who were unfavorable to adoption. They couldn't tell us whether that meant a longer wait or that we would never get Zachary.

"Oh, Lord, we are standing on a promise you gave us, so we'll fight in prayer for that promise. Help us to stand strong in this storm of disappointment and learn all you have for us." That was our continual prayer and hope.

During the delay, we kept busy doing the things God called us to. I went through training for the Pregnancy Resource Center that would soon open in our area. We learned even more about the risks and harms of abortion and how we could introduce better solutions than that destructive choice to women. My part in God's plan to help women and bring life to our community excited me.

Falling in Love with the Word

God solidified my foundation through Bible studies. One was Bible Study Fellowship (BSF), with Carole Gardner as the amazing teaching leader. She loved the Word of God, and it showed in her storytelling. She had a way about her that drew me into the pages of Scripture. I walked alongside the people she mentioned. I understood their trials and celebrated their joys. Carole spent thirty to forty hours a week preparing for the lecture, and the glow on her face and the journey she took us on as she taught reflected that time.

The Bible came alive, causing me to fall in love with the people on the pages. I learned how to read between the lines of Scripture and to experience life, feelings, and emotions with them.

One week Carole taught from the Old Testament book of Genesis, where it tells of Abraham's arising early the morning after the Lord told him to sacrifice his son Isaac. He didn't question God or change his mind. Instead of waiting around for a new word from God, he quickly obeyed and believed God would provide.

As Abraham and his son walked up the mountain, Isaac carried the wood. The picture represented Christ carrying his cross up the mountain for his own sacrificial death. How did Sarah feel while she waited back at the tent? Had Abraham shared with her what God had requested? Did she argue with Abraham and ask him not to do it? Did Sarah grieve, or did she choose to stand on God's promise that they would have many children? Scripture doesn't tell us, but as I put myself in the storyline, I could imagine Sarah's feelings.

Abraham trusted and obeyed. I thought of how I had sacrificed my own children on the altar of convenience and disobedience rather than rely on God. And now my loving Lord—the God of restoration and hope—was taking my sin of death and bringing life through the provision of a son.

The examples of those who went before us in Scripture instructed me how to walk through my own life. I have Carole to thank for my love of the Word and for my Bible knowledge.

Mentored by Godly Women

The Lord surrounded me with wonderful women who taught and mentored me during that time. They knew Jesus and loved him with all their hearts—and, boy, could they pray! We met for prayer at our church on Thursday nights. It wasn't the largest gathering, but it was mighty. Mary Bradley, Ann Marx, Ginny McGee, and Pat were regular attendees. I considered those special women as giants and generals for the Lord. They were instrumental in teaching me the power of the Word of God and how to pray it over specific situations.

Ann is one of the most humble, prayerful people I know. Mary is always positive and never has a negative thing to say. Ginny lived to pray and loved being in the presence of the Lord. It showed in the constant, glowing smile on her face. And Pat, well, you have read the powerful influence she has in my life.

Many nights only the five of us went, but God showed up every time. Some of those nights we went into the sanctuary and danced to worship music while singing of his goodness. During others we warred and interceded for souls to be saved and for people to receive their healing. We also prayed for our nation and other countries. The ladies expanded my vision and taught me that God desires we pray for others and not just ourselves. We witnessed God move in many ways, which strengthened our faith.

We also met at my house on Friday mornings—a wonderful time of discovery and growing in the power of prayer. I
learned that God does hear us. Our prayers are a sweet-smelling
incense to his nostrils. He delights when he hears his children's
voices as they speak his very words, believing those words
accomplish what they say.

Our church had a Bible study that met on Tuesday mornings. Those of us who participated grew in relationship with the
Lord and one another as we studied his Word and were trans-
parent with one another. We formed close friendships and truly
carried one another's burdens.

The Lord taught me through the Bible studies, prayer times,
and friendships to be a better Christ-follower. He put his heart's
desires within me, hid his Word in my heart, and transformed
me with his compassion and love. God prepared me for what
he had ahead in our lives by building my foundation and walls
with those precious jewels.

Within all of this, our love for the lost and our desire to see
the kingdom of God grow increased. We shared Christ with
those we met and knew.

Steve and I lived in a house at the end of a cul-de-sac, and
we witnessed the Lord work throughout our neighborhood. We
shared about Jesus with a family who lived two houses away.
They left a life of drug use and started attending church with
us. Todd and Dianne became some of our best friends. Dianne
came to prayer meetings and boldly asked God to reveal himself to her entire family and to our whole neighborhood. Not
too long afterward, several on our street came to know Jesus
and started attending church with us.

The Lord gave me the privilege of having a part in leading a
close friend from my past to salvation. He is now married to my
sister's best friend, and they serve as missionaries in another
country. God's ways fill me with wonder and delight.

Our Family Is Hit by a Storm

The Lord gave us amazing joys as we waited for Zachary, but there were also times of affliction and storms. A couple of months after we got Zachary's picture and were celebrating his arrival, we received devastating news.

On a brisk Saturday in March—my birthday—my mom underwent a bronchoscopy examination at the hospital. She had been experiencing upper back pain, just below her shoulders, and was coughing up blood. Mom had smoked for years but with God's help quit a year earlier.

Linda, her husband, Roger, and I waited while they did the procedure. Dad didn't join us because he mistakenly went to the wrong place. We watched as the medical team wheeled Mom out of surgery to take her back to her room. The serious look on the doctor's face caused us concern, so we asked if he could spare a minute and talk to us. "We found cancer," he said. He was blunt and short on details. "I want to talk to your mother before I say more."

"What did he just say?" Linda and I both mouthed the words as we looked at each other in shock.

Did he say she has cancer? That was a lot for my mind to grasp. Mom was young—only fifty-eight years old—and she seemed so healthy. My thoughts blurred together and took me to a not-so-good place. I imagined what life would be like without her.

Dad had a big job running the bakery, and Mom couldn't drive. If she needed chemotherapy treatments, who would take her? Who would care for her and do the chores around the house? Dad works long hours, and most of them are at night. Who would be with Mom during that time?

My head swirled with questions and confusion, and my emotions spun out of control, not knowing where to land. "God, please take this away," I pleaded. I hoped the doctor was wrong and that she'd be all right.

The oncologist planned a meeting with our family in Mom's hospital room to inform us about the type of cancer she had, discuss options and treatments, and answer our questions. All the siblings and some of our spouses were there to offer support. We wanted to fully understand what to expect in the days ahead and to help Mom and Dad make decisions. We tried to keep the talk light to avoid saying anything that would cause hopelessness, but apprehension occupied our minds. Our conversations were more like nervous chatter.

Life took a wrong turn, and we had no control over the direction it was headed. What do you do when there is nothing you can do? You pray and ask Jesus to fill every space in the situation. And sometimes you cry. I did all I could to hold back my tears because I didn't want Mom to see my unstable emotions. Everyone else in the room appeared to be doing the same.

Before our conference with her oncologist, Mom told us she didn't want chemotherapy. Too many people close to her had suffered through that.

The doctor entered the room and got right to the point. He said, "You have a fast-growing oat cell lung cancer. It's wrapped around your heart and is inoperable. The only treatment we can do is chemotherapy." We didn't like that news at all—especially since Mom had already given us her opinion about chemo.

"Your chances of survival aren't good," he continued. "Without chemo you will live only one to three months, and with the chemo your odds will increase. It'll buy you some time, but there are no guarantees."

We asked questions and brainstormed how we could pitch in to make it work. After hearing the doctor's prognosis and listening to our fears, Mom made the selfless decision to have chemotherapy. She heard our desperation and chose what was best for us, not her.

Enjoying the Time We Have

Steve had a new job position that required him to work long-distance—a six-month assignment. That allowed me to travel to my parents' home and take care of Mom during the week. I spent time with Steve on the weekends.

My sister Lisa lived three hours away and came on Saturdays and Sundays. Linda was closer to town, but she had two children, so she filled in as needed. We helped Mom with doctor appointments, cleaned the house, cooked the meals, and did other necessary tasks. Our plan involved doing what we could, and we asked God to do what we couldn't.

Watching Mom go through her treatments and trying to stay happy in the atmosphere of sickness and wilderness was hard, but I cherished the time I had with her and that outweighed the heaviness. I took her to chemo appointments. We'd often go shopping afterward. Sometimes, as we walked into the mall, she found the closest trash bin and threw up. Once she finished, we'd go on our way. She was such a trooper. Mom loved to get her Christmas shopping done before summer, so she was on a mission, and cancer was not going to deter her.

Mom and I had wonderful times together through that season. We read the Bible and did my BSF homework at the kitchen table. We had amazing conversations about the Lord and the things we were learning in his Word as we studied. I enjoyed every minute of having Mom all to myself.

I worked on projects around the house, some that she had wanted done for years but never had the time. One day she asked me to clean out all the kitchen cabinets. As I tackled them one by one, she told me what to keep and what to throw away.

The stories she told me about the dishes and treasures I found opened my heart to the past. I unburied a yellow teapot with gold trim from the back of a top cabinet. As I held it, memories of the tea parties she had with each of us girls when we were little flooded in. Those were special times. She filled the teapot with pop and gave us chocolate chips and marshmal-lows. We sipped from our dainty teacups as we sat and talked, pretending like we were all grown up and oh-so-sophisticated.

I stumbled upon a chocolate stash she had hidden in the back of one of the cabinets. We had a good laugh about that. Mom was still hiding goodies even after all of us kids were out of the house. She told me how she used to wait for us to go to bed, and in the quiet of the night she read, wrote in her journal, and ate chocolate.

What fun I had listening to her reminisce about our grow-ing-up years and hearing her thoughts of who we had become. And what a wonderful treasure the Lord gave me. Those moments with Mom were my precious stones of rubies, sap-phires, and turquoise. I didn't fully appreciate that time until years later.

On one particular day Mom and I watched *The 700 Club*. During the show, the host gave a word of knowledge that someone was being healed of lung cancer. We looked at each other, and I said, "Let's grab hands and claim and agree with this word of healing over you." She agreed and we prayed. I hid that word in my heart and brought it to the Lord many times in the days ahead.

Mom began to feel a bit better, and tests showed the cancer was shrinking. I held on tightly to God's Word and declared according to the promise in Isaiah 53:5 that by his stripes Mom was healed.

One day, when Mom felt pretty good, we went to the bakery and pulled down some out-of-control grape vines that were damaging the awning in the back. We hauled them home and spent the next couple of days making beautiful wreaths.

My very creative mother loved to draw and paint. Many of her paintings hung on the walls of our home. She wrote pages and pages of poetry. Her artistry also showed in the way she dressed and in how beautiful our home was decorated. She had a flair for style.

As I spent time with Mom and saw her giftedness, I realized that I got my passion for drawing, decorating, and music from her. We were similar in many ways, even in our appearance. She used to look at me seriously and say, "Luana, you and I have the same Roman noses. They are roaming all over our faces." Then we'd laugh.

Moving to the Next Season

After six months, Steve's out-of-town assignment ended. Because we had been separated so long, I came home to spend time with him. Lisa, Linda, and Lynette filled those missing spots in the schedule. We came up on weekends when we could, or I tried to come during the week.

We jumped back into the routine of our life. I had several speaking engagements with Aglow and pro-life organizations. I attended my prayer groups and Bible studies. Steve and I were able to continue in the leadership roles we had at church, and life seemed to get somewhat back to normal.

During all that, we were still waiting to hear when the Indian government would allow Zachary and the other children to come to the states. My heart desired to hold Zachary as a baby and to experience the beginning of his life. I longed to snuggle with him when he drank a bottle, to hear his first words, and to see his first steps. But in a few months he would turn two, and we had not yet laid eyes on him, much less been able to cuddle and play.

More than a year had passed since Mom was diagnosed, and we were blessed to have her still with us. I had kept that word in my heart and reminded God often for her healing. She started to have new symptoms and underwent more tests. The tests revealed that the cancer had spread, so they treated the affected areas with radiation. Because of the severity of pain and horrific side effects from treatment, the doctor increased her medications, and she slept a lot.

Dad sold the bakery, and he and Linda became Mom's primary caregivers. Lisa continued to come on weekends when she could. My brother, Larry, and his wife, Cindy, as well as Steve and I and Lynette, came when we could. Leslie lived in Texas and wasn't able to get home very often.

The storm came back with vengeance and tossed our family about. Looking back on that time now, I see similarities to the story in Matthew 8 when the disciples were in a boat on the lake with Jesus. A furious storm threatened to overturn their boat, and the disciples cried out for the Lord to save them. They thought they were going to drown.

I'm sure our family and the disciples experienced many of the same feelings and our questions were probably much alike. "Lord, where are you?" "Are you asleep in the bottom of the boat?" "Do you see the raging winds and crashing waves?" "Will you come rebuke the storm and speak peace to our troubled hearts?" "God I trust you. You see the whole picture and you hold us all in your hands. I surrender my emotions and thoughts and ask you to press in close as we go through this storm."

§

Questions to Ponder

We started this chapter with Isaiah 54:11-12: "Afflicted city, lashed by storms and not comforted, I will rebuild you with stones of turquoise, your foundations with lapis lazuli. I will make your battlements of rubies, your gates of sparkling jewels, and all your walls of precious stones."

Oh, favored one of God, do you feel like that storm-tossed city, beaten on every side, and you just can't find comfort or peace anywhere?

What are you praying for and believing God for that is not being answered?

How can you sing and find joy in this hard situation?

I encourage you to continue to stand on the Word of God. Find those Scriptures that apply to your situation and life, and begin to declare them out loud. As you speak them they will become truth and life to you. They will bring you hope and allow you to "sing in your wilderness." That is where you'll find relief.

The Lord loves you so much and wants his best for you. We live in a broken and fallen world where pain and disappointment seem to beat up on us. But we do not serve a broken or fallen God.

He is always faithful, even when things don't go as expected. Stand on and believe in the promises he has given you in his Word. He will turn all things for your good. If he says it, he will do it. God pledges to build new foundations from precious stones. He will turn your sadness into joy and your mourning into dancing.

Here's truth: God loves you with an everlasting love. He is love. In 1 Corinthians 13, God says love never fails. Love always protects, always trusts, always hopes, and always perseveres. Now we look through the glass dimly—the reflection in the mirror is puzzling. We know only in part, but the day will come when we understand it fully.

We have human perspective in our lives, but God has the heavenly perspective. When we know he loves us, we can trust him to work for our good. Remember the truth of his Word, and when life is hard, you can fall on him and cry on his shoulder. He will be there to catch you and wrap his arms around you, giving you everything you need. As Proverbs 3:5 emphasizes, we don't have to understand; we just have to trust.

Let's come in agreement together on the Lord's word for your life.

§

Prayer

Father, we love you so much, and we trust you in every aspect of our lives. You are always working for our good, so we bring you all of our pain and sorrows and ask that you use them as building stones for the purposes you have for us.

Lord, we declare that you sent your Word to heal us and that by your stripes we are healed. We use that Word as our sword and we wield it at all sickness in our body and our loved ones' bodies. We declare that all sickness is defeated and destroyed. It is cursed at its root, and the healing power of the Lord Jesus Christ rules and reigns now in its place. We declare we are the healed in Jesus' name.

Lord, we bring to you those things we have been asking for. You say you give us the desires of our hearts. Those desires are yours. You planted them within us, so we give them back to you. We know we can trust you with them.

We will patiently wait on you, Lord, and continually stand in the place of faith and trust. Show us if there are things we need to do or pursue for those dreams and desires to come to pass. We know in this process of waiting that you are building trust and character in us. You are fashioning us into precious jewels that will reflect your image as you turn us in your hand.

Lord, you say that the prayers of a righteous man avail and accomplish much, so we believe that and will be on watch for your will to manifest. We also thank you for filling us with your perfect peace and comfort during our difficult times. We love you so much and long to be a fortified city that shines its light for all to see. We ask this in Jesus' name, amen.

7. Established in Righteousness

"All your children will be taught by the Lord, and great will be their peace. In righteousness you will be established."
(Isaiah 54:13–14)

October had come and the 29th would be Zachary's second birthday. We received a phone call from Love Basket and learned that the Indian government had new judges. They planned to release the children who were approved for adoption, and they'd arrive in the United States on November 7, which was just weeks away. It seemed like we had so much to do to get ready. The children would fly into St. Louis, and we would take our new son home from the airport.

We spread the word to our friends and family who prayed for us during our adoption process. They were excited, and many wanted to go with us to welcome him. When you carry something in prayer for so long, you become part of that birthing and delivery room answer. Our friends held Zachary in their hearts like we had, and they witnessed their prayers grow into a reality. Together we were family and adopting a son.

The day before his scheduled arrival, we received another phone call from Love Basket. They informed us that a bomb scare in Bombay, India, had delayed the flight for twenty-four hours. Zachary would now arrive on November 8, a day later than originally planned. Again we had to wait, but our gratitude for his safety surpassed our disappointment. In biblical numerology, eight is the number for new beginnings. Zachary's middle name, Naveen, meant new beginnings. The Lord gave us peace that he was present and in control of the situation.

Zachary's Homecoming

When the day finally came to meet our son, we all loaded into a rented motor home and headed to St. Louis to celebrate Zachary's homecoming. Our friend Don White drove most of the five-hour trip. That way we could enjoy and savor God's miracle in our lives. Linda and her adopted children, Nathan and Yenae, as well as my sister-in-law, Cindy, and her four-month-old daughter, Stacie, came along. Our neighbor Dianne joined us with her five-year-old daughter, Amber, to observe our amazing answer to prayer. I will forever be grateful to Dianne for sharing Amber with me so many times when I longed for a child.

Our pastor, Rick McReynolds, and his wife, Beth, came to support us, in addition to many others from our church. Pat had arranged for a surprise baby shower on the trip down. Opening presents, laughing, and sharing our exciting time with everyone brought Steve and me great joy and fun memories that will last forever. It also helped that long drive go much quicker.

After we arrived in St. Louis, we ate dinner with the staff of Love Basket and the other adoptive parents. They gave us instructions for the evening and took pictures, and we were off to the airport for our new arrivals.

This happened in 1990 before the September 11 attacks, so we all hovered around the gate as the plane landed, hoping for a glimpse of our children. As the housemother from the orphanage walked down the sky bridge with all the kids clinging to her, Steve and I immediately recognized Zachary. We had seen only three pictures of him, but he had taken up residence in our hearts. The bond already in place with that curly, black-haired boy with beautiful, big brown eyes was unexplainable.

As with all new parents, we delighted in every part we saw of our new son. He had two little hands with five little fingers on each one. He had two little feet. Much tinier than most two-year-olds, he looked so tired and scared. I pried him away from his grip on the housemother, wrapped my arms around him, and whisked him off to the bathroom. He cried, kicked, and clawed. My mother's heart broke for this child with an unstable life. I had just torn him away from the only security he knew.

The adoption agency warned us that would happen, but I couldn't help but wonder what was going through Zachary's mind. Linda followed me to the bathroom, where we changed his dirty diaper and dressed him in fresh clothes. Forty-eight hours in the same outfit made for a stinky boy. We checked his scalp and curly locks, as we had been directed. No lice. After we got him cleaned up, I held him tight. He surrendered to my embrace and buried his head into my chest. We snuggled for the rest of the trip home.

Zachary lifted his head only once to look at the strangers surrounding him. He appeared to be thirsty, so I handed him a half-filled cup. When he put it to his mouth, he tilted it, and the contents spilled down his face and front. The information we received from the agency said he no longer took a bottle, so I wondered why he didn't know how to drink properly. Later we learned that the liquid we all take for granted was in short supply at the orphanage. Rather than allowing the kids unlimited drinking privileges, they lined them up several times a day and poured water into their wide-open mouths with a ladle. That explained why he tipped his head all the way back as he drank.

Zachary Meets the Family

We got home late that Thursday night. Early the next morning, Dad called and said Mom wasn't doing well. Linda and Cindy returned to our parents' house immediately to help and to console Dad. Steve had to go into work, so we planned to leave right after he got off.

We had been told to make Zachary's life as consistent as we could. They wanted us to gradually take him from rice and curry to an American diet. His eating and bedtimes should be as regular as possible, and we were advised to not overload him with new places and people too soon. So far, we weren't off to a good start.

We packed a bag and headed out of town to join my family at Mom's and Dad's. With all the people and activity there, consistency in mealtimes and bedtimes was out of the question. We did the best we could, but the chaos made scheduling anything out of our control. We hoped that once we returned home we'd be able to fall into a routine.

Mom slept most of the weekend, waking only on a few occasions. One of those times was when I came into the room to introduce her to her new grandson. Her eyes fluttered open, and she said, "I knew it. He's beautiful." Then she went back to sleep.

Another moment was when I sat at her bedside and had just finished reading the last words in Psalm 23—"and I will dwell in the house of the Lord forever." She awakened and thanked me.

On Sunday night, we packed up and returned home. I didn't want to leave, but Steve had to work on Monday, and Zachary needed a sense of normalcy.

Mom's Homecoming

Early Tuesday morning, Dad called to say Mom had passed away. I was numb. I knew the situation looked bad, but I still believed in the miracle of her healing. How was this possible? How could death have pushed its way in and stolen the gift of life God gave us through Zachary?

It was as if Mom's and Zachary's lives kissed and then headed in different directions. Mom wouldn't get to experience her new grandchild, and Zachary wouldn't get to know the amazing woman who prayed big prayers on his behalf before ever meeting him face to face. None of it made sense.

We packed and headed out of town—again. And again our friends provided encouragement and strength. The same people who prayed Zachary home knelt before God's throne and prayed for our peace during that painful and difficult time.

Dianne babysat Zachary and some of my siblings' children during Mom's visitation. Many from our church made the hour-long drive for the visitation and funeral to show support and to pray for us. Pat stayed overnight and watched Zachary during the funeral, and Don came to sit with our family, reminding us what our mother and family had meant to him.

Through our friends, the Lord showcased his great love for us. I had never experienced anything like that before—complete selflessness and so much giving. In the midst of such heartbreak, loss, and pain, an indescribable peace cradled me.

I had so many questions—and I especially didn't understand why God didn't heal Mom—but I knew he was right there with us. He carried us and comforted us through it. Because he continued to prove his faithfulness, trustworthiness, and goodness, I left my unknowns in his loving hands.

A couple of days before she died, Mom told Lynette about her journals. One of them contained letters telling what she had bequeathed to each of us. They were in a dining room hutch, and she wanted Lynette to find them so we could read what she had to say.

Lynette located the journals after Mom was gone. Although written when we were young, each entry was perfectly tailored to who we had become. In the quietness of late evenings after she put us to bed, Mom wrote the prophetic words that we would treasure forever.

A year after Mom's death, my BSF friend Janet Huber took a portion of each letter, printed it in calligraphy, and framed it. I gave each of my siblings their framed letter for Christmas that year.

Here is Mom's message to me:

Dear Luana,

To you I bequeath the desire to be liked and the capacity for liking back. An ability to make friends and laughter that bubbles and makes you want to bottle it. Like all my other children, a certain moodiness that plagues you at times, and blesses you at others. Also, the talent of intuition, a certain knowing without rhyme or reason. To you, the ability to talk and express yourself well. A certain self-confidence that makes you feel attractive, and then does make you so, even in other people's eyes.

The talent of warming your way into other people's hearts and getting what you want, not selfishly, but with a willingness to return that love tenfold.

To you also goes a sense of justice and unprejudice. To you a deep need for human love and closeness, and because of this you will always be aware of other peoples' need for the same.

You are maturing and unfolding into a very lovely and unselfish person with the awareness of the world around you.

You have the talent for taking things as they come and in the end, not letting them devastate you, but picking yourself up and trying again. This will see you through many hard and sorrowful times.

Love you forever,

Mom

I thank God for his amazing outpouring of love during that difficult time. That love sustained us as we transitioned into a different season of life without my mother and with a new child.

Getting Back to Normal?

After we returned home, our goal was to get Zachary into a routine and settled into his own space and bed. He had been through a lot already, and so many other things had taken our attention in the last month. We wanted him to have stability and to know how deeply we cared for him.

We could only imagine what Zachary's perspective and thoughts were. At just two years old, he had been ripped from everything he knew. He was thousands of miles away from his home country with no familiar faces. The people he lived with had white skin. They spoke a funny language. Their food tasted strange. The climate was different. And the list goes on. We wanted to make his upheaval as comfortable as possible.

On the first day home, I cooked rice and curry and placed it on the table in front of him, proud of myself for cooking it for the first time. I was excited to see his reaction to the food he loved. He looked at the bowl, looked at me, and pushed it away as if to say, "Are you kidding me? I've had pizza, pasta, and cookies, and now you want me to go back to eating this?" He then turned to me with a questioning gaze, probably wanting to ask, "So what's for lunch?" The rice and curry took a lot of time to make, but I had to laugh.

I'm amazed at how resilient and adaptable children are. Zachary learned things quickly and was a very contented and loving child. He had lost his sense of security, though, and didn't want to let go of me for the first couple of months he was with us. That presented a few problems. One is that he had never seen men before, and they scared him. He screamed if Steve came near him. If I needed to go somewhere, Zac sat by the door and cried until I returned.

Steve desperately wanted children to cuddle and love, so he was heartbroken when Zachary wouldn't allow him to come close or hold him. On many nights, Steve quietly tiptoed into Zachary's room after he fell asleep and picked him up from his bed to snuggle and pray over him. Yes, we had numerous obstacles to overcome, but our loving, wise God helped us every step of the way.

We established a consistent pattern for sleeping, meals, baths, and other weekly routines. Every Sunday we went to church as a family. We put Zachary in the nursery, where he learned to trust others and make friends. Many Sundays they had to take me out of the worship service because Zac cried or wasn't playing well with others. But each week he became more at home and more assured that we would never leave him.

Eventually, Zachary learned to appreciate Steve's presence in his life. He ran toward him with arms outstretched like other boys run toward their father, and my heart soared as I thought about the many beautiful miracles God had worked in our family. Hearing Zachary delightedly call out, "Daddy!" while pointing at Steve made all of the struggles and heartache worth it.

Zachary got to know those who prayed for him, and they became a part of his life. He made good friends and playmates at church while also learning the Word of God and how much Jesus loved him.

Zachary and I also went to BSF on Thursdays. In class, he cried and caused disruptions. It was another difficult adjustment for both of us, and just staying home would have been easier. But two precious godly leaders, Kate Moulton and Nancy Mappin, held Zachary and prayed over him without ever complaining about his behavior. They poured into him—and doted on him—as if he were theirs.

Nancy gave Zachary Big Red Gum. Not only did it become a comfort to him, it was also a common bond they shared. Still today, he holds a special place in his heart for Kate, Nancy, Big Red Gum, and all those who played such an important part during that time in his life.

Zachary marvels at all of his "aunts" and "uncles," as he warmly refers to them. I'll never be able to adequately thank the countless people who came alongside of Steve and me to help us graciously transition Zachary back to security and into his destiny.

It wasn't easy or without complications, but we began to settle into a new normal. Christmas was upon us, and it would be our first experience with our own child coming downstairs to discover presents under the tree. We had mixed emotions— excitement to share the season's joys with Zachary, yet sadness that we had to do it without my mother. Everything was so different. But that's the way life is at times, isn't it?

First Christmas with Zachary and without Mom

We arranged to go to Dad's house, as did the rest of my siblings. We didn't want Dad to be alone, plus we wanted to have everyone together for Zac's first Christmas celebration. The house was filled with lots of noise and activity, and even though it had been only a month since we last saw each other, we received encouragement in being assembled again.

When we searched the storage area for the Christmas tree and decorations, we found bags of wrapped presents Mom had purchased for all of us. She made sure we had gifts as a reminder of her love for us. After we strung the lights on the tree and hung every ornament in place, we positioned Mom's angel at the top. We took a step back to admire our creation, and although it was beautiful, it didn't compare to how perfectly she always decorated it. We tucked the presents under the tree with care, as Mom would. And on Christmas morning, we rejoiced in our cherished memories.

Zachary appeared overwhelmed with so many gifts. It was all new to him. He didn't have playthings at the orphanage in India—only sticks and rocks and whatever his imagination came up with. Puzzled with the toy cars, he held them in his little hand and spun the wheels with his fingers. He cocked his head and studied them for a while. We could almost see the questions whirling in his mind. What joy and delight we had as we watched him! It was probably more fun for us than it was for him as he received and unwrapped presents for the first time.

His first Christmas was a good one. Zachary got to know his cousins and aunts much better, and he became more comfortable with all of us.

More Kisses from Heaven

In the weeks to come, we helped Dad sort through Mom's things. Some of her clothes went to my sisters and me; others we saved for a garage sale, and the rest we took to Goodwill. We went through jewelry, pictures, and her other personal items. One minute we laughed at the fun times we had with her, and the next minute we cried about what we missed.

While going through her sketchbooks and paintings, we found another treasure. Mom valued people of every culture, and she taught us to never have prejudices on the basis of outward appearance. She told us to look at a person's heart. Her love for others showed in her many portraits. She rarely painted landscapes. As we collected her artwork, we found precious pearls of her heart. Two specific paintings stood out.

One portrayed a small Asian girl who held a bowl containing chopsticks. She wore a red outfit and had a haircut similar to Linda's son, Nathan. That astounded us, because Linda and Roger had two adopted Asian children. Their son, Nathan, and daughter, Yenae, both came from Korea.

The second painting showcased an Indian woman praying. A beautiful green headdress accompanied her white sari, and she had a black dot in the middle of her forehead. Steve and I adopted Zachary from India.

How did Mom know she would have grandchildren from those countries? She painted the pictures years before knowing Linda and I couldn't have children and would choose to adopt.

I truly believe Mom heard the voice of God and saw our children long before they existed. How many times had she prayed for them and declared the plans and purposes of God over each of their lives? Were they in our care because Mom came into agreement with heaven for their destinies? Did she ponder that secret in her heart, even as Virgin Mary did of the Child she carried from the Lord?

We will never know the answer to those questions, but it makes me mindful of Psalm 139:16, which says, "You **saw** me before I was born. Every day of my life was recorded in your book. Every moment was laid out before a single day had passed" (NLT, emphasis mine).

In Jeremiah 1:4 God tells Jeremiah, "I **knew** you before I formed you in your mother's womb. Before you were born I set you apart and appointed you as my prophet to the nations" (NLT, emphasis mine).

God knows the plans he has for us before we're born. Why wouldn't he share those secrets and mysteries with those who partner in prayer with him to bring them to pass? I believe Mom had prophetic revelation in her heart, and that's why she said, "I knew it. He's beautiful" when she awakened to see Zachary for the first time. She knew because she had already seen him in the Spirit. God had shown her.

Mom's doll collection provided even more confirmation of her prophetic revelation. Most of them were girls, but a certain one was a boy. An Eastern Indian boy. She also had two Korean dolls. If you guessed one boy and one girl, you're right.

God is an amazing God. He tells his friends his intentions, and he whispers his secrets into their hearts. Linda and I have those paintings hanging on our walls. The dolls have specific spots on our shelves. They serve as a reminder of God's plans for our lives and his special love.

§

Questions to Ponder

Think of a time when God revealed himself to you in a personal way.

Are you listening carefully for his voice? Or are you caught up in the circumstances around you and missing what he has to say?

Are you mourning the loss of someone and in need of comfort? As you listen, what do you hear the Lord say to you?

Oh, beloved of the Lord, whatever your questions or concerns, God cares. He longs to spend time with you. He wants you to lay your head on his chest and hear his heart beat for you. He desires to dance and celebrate with you, rejoicing in all that you are.

When you awaken in the morning, he's right there with you, waiting to hear your voice. Each day he offers new mercies for you, urging you to grab hold of them and apply them to your shortfalls. He yearns for you to take his hand and walk side by side with him on the path he created just for you.

Will you trust him? He is trustworthy. Will you cry out to him and share your hurts and pains? Will you allow him to mend, heal, and comfort you?

The God of the universe wants an intimate relationship with you. He loves you because he is love. First Corinthians 13:4–7 gives us a definition of love, and in doing so gives us a description of God. Here's my paraphrase of the verses: "God is patient and kind. God is not jealous or boastful or proud or rude. God does not demand his own way. God is not irritable, and he keeps no record of being wronged. God does not rejoice about injustice, but he rejoices whenever the truth wins out. God never gives up on you and never loses faith in you. He is always hopeful about you, and he endures through every circumstance concerning you."

Let him love you like only he can do.

I encourage you to sit before the Lord with your eyes closed and chat with him about your heart's desires. Discuss the losses you've been through. Share any feelings of abandonment with him. Cry before him and just be real. Let Jesus bathe you in his healing balm. Allow his cleansing water to wash your burdens and pains away.

As your eyes are still closed, ask God to show you where he is and what he has for you. Your mind thinks in pictures, so trust the Lord to place an image in your mind of what he wants you to see. That's another way he communicates with us. Write your revelations in a journal. He may take you to a beautiful place and talk with you. Perhaps he'll place a gift in your hand or give you something meaningful. As you spend time with him, he will bring healing to your soul. Those moments with him will forever be in your memory, and you will be able to draw life from them again and again.

Let me pray for you as you spend time with him.

§

Prayer

Oh, gracious Father, thank you for saving and rescuing us. Thank you for how you love us and long to be with us. Lord, I pray for those who are coming before you now. Reveal yourself to them so they will see the abundance of love, grace, and mercy you have for them. Let them walk along the shores of the sea of forgetfulness with you, throwing in all that needs to be forgiven and blotted out.

Father, take them to a meaningful place—your marvelous place of healing and restoration. Let them hear your voice and feel your touch. I know one moment with you can transform us, so I ask for that moment for these dear ones seeking you now.

Baptize them in your love and clothe them in the garments of praise for their spirit of heaviness. Let them run and dance with you in your courts of praise. Lord, I ask that you give each one a gift and allow them to open and see what you have divinely and uniquely created for them. Thank you for drawing these precious ones into a new and closer relationship with you. Love them as only you can do.

Lord, I declare the prayer in Ephesians 3 over these readers. I pray that out of your glorious riches you will strengthen them with power through your Spirit in their inner being, so you will dwell in their hearts through faith. I pray that they are being rooted and established in your love and have power to grasp how wide and long and high and deep is your love for them. Jesus, help them to know this love that surpasses knowledge—that they may be filled to the measure of all the fullness of God.

Now to him who is able to do immeasurably more than all we ask or imagine, according to his power that is at work within us. To him be the glory. Amen.

8. A New Weapon Created

*"See, it is I who created the blacksmith who fans the coals
into flame and forges a weapon fit for its work. And it
is I who have created the destroyer to wreak havoc."*
(Isaiah 54:16)

I marvel at the way the Lord works in our lives. Although
it doesn't make sense to us, he weaves our trials and our
joys into a beautiful tapestry that portrays an amazing work of
art and brings him glory. Just as a builder has a blueprint for
his finished work, God always has a plan.

The verse in Isaiah above reminds us that God uses the
obstacles and struggles in our lives. He is the blacksmith who
fans the flames of difficulty, and out of that fire emerges an
expertly formed and crafted weapon that God can use to defeat
the enemy.

A Call from Heaven

At the time of Zachary's arrival and Mom's death, life
became like a whirlwind. We made arrangements for Mom's
funeral and went right into Thanksgiving and Christmas. We
helped care for Dad, acclimated Zachary to his new home, and

went through Mom's things. Within all our busyness, I hadn't fully processed everything that happened. I hadn't mourned for Mom, nor had I celebrated God's gift of Zachary.

One night as I sat in bed alone and talked to God, I thanked him for Zachary and Steve, our friends, and all he had given us. With a heart overflowing with gratitude, I picked up the phone to call Mom. I wanted to share my feelings of joy with her. Then I realized she was gone and I'd never be able speak with her again. I wouldn't be able to chat about the exciting moments or the hard times. She's the one who had always given me advice and prayed with me. As the reality of losing her set in, I started to have a meltdown.

She wasn't just my mom—she was my friend, my prayer partner, and even my counselor at times. Zachary wouldn't have her in his life. He would never get to know his grandma.

My tears came in waves. I wept for what seemed like hours, and I couldn't shake myself out of it. I unloaded my sorrows and concerns to God and told him how much I loved him. "I know you love me too, Lord, but I need my mommy right now." The ache in my heart was almost too much to bear. I longed for her to wrap her arms around me and tell me that everything would be okay. "Please, God, hold me," I sobbed. "I need your touch."

Steve worked third shift, so I couldn't cling to him for comfort. It was two o'clock in the morning; waking Zachary just to nuzzle him was out of the question. Curled in a fetal position on the bed, I continued to convulse my prayers to God, and my phone rang. *Who could it possibly be at this time of the morning?* I ran as fast as I could to grab it so Zac wouldn't wake up. "Hello," I said in a hushed voice.

The voice on the other end of the line was quiet too. It was Pat, and she was concerned. "Are you all right?" she whispered. "God woke me up and told me to call you." She told me about her struggle with his request. "I said, 'Are you serious, Lord? It's two a.m. People are asleep at that time of the day.'" Pat said she even brushed her teeth, hoping she could get out of it if she stalled. But because of the Lord's insistence, she obeyed and called me. She wondered why it was so urgent.

God had heard my prayers and quickly answered them. I was in awe of his compassion and how intimately he loved me. Through my sobs I told Pat about the grief that caused my meltdown. She came over, and we prayed and wept while holding each other. I know the Lord had his arms around both of us in that moment, completing the circle of love.

Ecclesiastes 4:12 says, "A person standing alone can be attacked and defeated, but two can stand back-to-back and conquer. Three are even better, for a triple-braided cord is not easily broken" (NLT).

Who is this God who is so personal, whose heart breaks for his children and longs to embrace them? This God who actually woke my friend from sleep so she would call and comfort me? He is real and alive. He hears every word we speak and knows every thought we think. He cares for our every hurt. Yes, God is always for us, so who can possibly be against us? Greater is the God who is in us than he who is in the world.

That night God forged a weapon of faith in me that established an even greater trust in him. I will never wonder again if God hears my prayers or if he cares about the difficult things I undergo. He proved to me in a very real way that he does. He will never leave me alone and will always be by my side.

The Weapons of Prayer and Friendships

God walked with me through many pits and fires. He was at work molding me into a sharp, precise weapon that could break down prison doors, cut through heavy chains, and retrieve the spoils he had already won.

He used prayer and ministry to shape me. I had the joy of meeting Kate McGovern, a woman who lived in a place of prayer. Although we didn't know each other, we discovered we had a history.

My two friends Michel and Kathy had gone with me to a Kay Arthur training class where we learned how to teach the Bible. Michel had a friend—Kate McGovern—who offered to host a Bible study in her home if we taught it. Our first gathering at her house started with introductions. One of the ladies said, "I'm Inggie Digman, and I'm from your hometown."

My dad had a friend named Eldon Digman, so I made a mental note to ask Inggie later if Eldon was her dad. After the study ended, I connected with her in the kitchen. "Yes, Eldon's my dad. How do you know him?"

"My dad is Paul Hoppman. He owned Paul's Pastry Shoppe in our hometown."

She let out a screech. "Paul made my wedding cake!"

Kate turned around abruptly and said, "Paul made my wedding cake too." We were all astounded.

Not only did we learn that the three of us were from the same hometown, but we also discovered that our parents were friends. The more we talked, the more we found many things in common. Kate's parents had close ties with my parents, and her mother attended two of the same prayer groups as my mom. I knew Kate's mom, Marie, well but had never met her daughters. We had so much fun sharing and laughing about the sweet surprise God had uncovered for us. That was the beginning of a fruitful and lasting relationship for Kate and me.

The Power of Prayer

Kate had a prayer group in her home every Friday morning (and still does). As we assembled there, we sensed God's presence in a big way. Every week was different. We'd go to the throne room without fail and declare what God says is ours to have.

Some weeks we performed prophetic acts as the Lord would lead us. Other weeks we lay on the floor and wept, and at times we sang and danced in his presence. Once, we got out a map of the United States, prayed over our nation, and blew the shofar.

One week the Lord told Raymond, a friend, to bring a loaf of bread and grape juice, and we had communion. People brought their instruments, and we praised and worshiped God for the entire time. Several we prayed for were healed of cancer, and one man's deaf ears began to hear. We prayed for a baby who had a hole in her heart. The next week, we heard that the doctors were baffled because tests showed a new heart.

Fridays became one of my favorite days. I expected the Lord to show up in power, and he always did. Those prayer meetings honed and sharpened us to be mighty weapons for the kingdom of God.

The Weapon of Ministry

In ministry, God often takes us back to our places of struggle—the prisons from which we received deliverance. Because we broke through the chains of addiction, abortion, abuse, or other bondages—and conquered their hold over us— we have (and know) the power to help bring others out.

Our new Pregnancy Resource Center had opened, and I volunteered as a receptionist and peer counselor. I loved that ministry because it aligned with my passion. My heart ached for the women who came in thinking they had no choice but to abort. Many were in a state of brokenness and hopelessness. I had the opportunity to pray with them and educate them on all their options.

I'm convinced that no woman wants to kill her child by abortion. She feels trapped and desperate and thinks no alternatives exist. As she searches for answers, she's sold a mound of lies and is convinced that disposing of her "clump of cells" is the only way out of her bleak situation. She takes the bait the deceiver throws at her and chooses the easy path. "It's a quick fix to my desperation," she tells herself. Then she's thrown into a deeper pit with even more devastating repercussions.

It was gut-wrenching for me when women came to the center and still chose abortion after knowing they would face more pain and trauma in their future. But I had no greater joy than when they chose life for their child. Children are miracles.

We had huge celebrations when moms returned to introduce us to their saved-from-abortion babies. We watched as those women beamed with delight while holding their little miracles. It seemed as if all their fears had faded away.

In time, we added an abstinence program at the center. My friend Cyndy Pollenteir and I helped develop the curriculum, and we called it W.A.I.T.—"With Abstinence I'm Treasured." It taught young people to wait for marriage before becoming sexually active. We went to schools, churches, and youth groups, emphasizing to the youth that they were valuable and worth waiting for.

Speaking to youth is one of my favorite things to do because they are so honest and candid. We heard it all and had so much fun with them. They called us "the sex ladies." At the end of our sessions we invited them to sign a pledge to the Lord to remain pure until their wedding night. We told them they could present it to their spouse as their gift on the day they got married.

Knowing your spouse waited for you because they valued the covenant of marriage and their partner is the greatest wedding gift anyone could have. Several people have told me about how they stayed pure until marriage after signing that pledge in high school. It always warms my heart when I hear those stories and know that God touched lives as we spoke.

The Weapon of Healing Brings Life

The Pregnancy Resource Center started a post-abortion Bible study. I was excited about that because I wanted all

God had for me. I also wanted to learn how to minister to other women hurt by abortion. The class was impressive and extremely beneficial.

Several people participated, so we didn't feel alone or like we were the only one who had committed the sin of abortion. That in itself was comforting. The eight-week course took us on a journey of restoration and freedom one step at a time. I was astonished to learn that the Lord had already walked me through many of the steps of healing.

We asked God to reveal the gender and names of our children. We sought out who we needed to forgive, wrote them letters asking for their forgiveness, and then burned the letters. The Lord confirmed to me again that he was definitely present in the process he was taking me through.

Fanning Flames at Rachel's Vineyard

The Lord sharpened me through my post-abortion redemption journey. I received healing not only through the Bible study at the Pregnancy Resource Center, but I was also blessed to go on a life-changing Rachel's Vineyard Retreat.[8]

My friends Ann and Tracy attended with me, and Tracy was part of the leadership team. The retreat was incredibly effective, causing us to go deeper into the Lord's forgiveness for our abortions. The most significant time of the intensely emotional weekend for me was the memorial service for our children. We were told to ask the Lord how he wanted us to remember them. We could write a poem or prayer for our child, or whatever we sensed God telling us. The Lord immediately gave me an idea, and I ran to a nearby store to get the items I needed.

The next day we gathered in a beautiful church in the hills of North Carolina for the ceremony. The entire front of the church

---

[8] I encourage you to visit the Rachel's Vineyard website and register for a retreat at www.rachelsvineyard.org.

was glass, which allowed us to see the grandiose, almost-mountainous, rolling hills. The trees reached to the sky as if they were praising the Lord, and the magnificent wildflowers danced in their vivid colors. Sunshine broke through the puffy clouds in the brilliant blue sky, showing off its light and power. The mesmerizing scene before us was like a glorious piece of art the Lord had painted just for us.

As the service got underway, we read Scriptures and sang. When we got to the portion where we were supposed to get up one by one and honor our children, each person walked to the front and read or sang a song to their aborted child. It was emotional, and we shed many tears.

The somber atmosphere in the room made me get more and more uncomfortable. I thought maybe I had misread God's nudges. Finally, when I was the only one left, I rose to take my place. I had hidden the items I bought at the store in the front of the church, so I quickly retrieved them. I emerged with a birthday cake, candles, hats, and party favors because I felt the Lord wanted us to celebrate the birthdays we had missed with our children.

For so many years I had mourned my babies. Now I was ready to celebrate their being in God's care and one day getting to see them. The sadness and grief in the air dissipated in that moment. Everyone jumped to their feet, put on party hats, and grabbed noisemakers. We lit the candles, sang "Happy Birthday" to our children, and ate cake in memory of all of them. What a way to stomp on the enemy's head! Yes, it was vindication for the tears we shed.

That weekend gave me a greater passion to see women healed and set free from the pain of abortion.

Living the Passion

My friend Elle Roetzel also had an abortion and shared my passion for life, so we began to teach an abortion-recovery

Bible study. The Lord allowed us the honor of encouraging many women toward freedom and victory. We watched as they recognized their value in God's eyes and realized his forgiveness and love for them. As women came out of their cells of shame and hopelessness, God gave us a glimpse in the Spirit of chains breaking and falling to the ground.

From leading the classes, a special bond developed between Elle and me. Our friendship and the fruit it produced were more plunder taken from the enemy's camp. Elle wrote a book giving God the glory for the spoils she has recovered in her life.

If you are a woman who has been hurt by abortion, I encourage you again to reach out to a Pregnancy Resource Center in your city and go through an abortion-recovery class. Even if you believe you're okay or that you're healed, it never hurts to receive more of what the Lord has for you. His well is deep and full. Drink from it in excess and be overwhelmed by his loving benefits.

§

Questions to Ponder

Oh, beloved of God, will you ask the Lord how he wants to use you as a weapon in his hand to destroy the works of the enemy and bring glory to him?

Can you think of a time you saw God work in brilliant and majestic ways? When?

How can you be a friend who hears God for others and reveals the glory of God to a lost and dying world?

The Lord longs to show us who he is. He wants to work in powerful ways in our lives. In our humanness, we limit him and have a skewed vision of his ability. He wants to raise us up on eagle's wings so we can run and not grow weary, to walk and not faint. He wants us to soar high above our natural perspective and view things from a supernatural position. Things look entirely different when we see them through the eyes of the Lord's compassion and love. Let's mount the back of that heavenly eagle and fly over our problems and concerns. We'll discover how small they are compared to God's bigness.

§

Prayer

Lord, I pray for heavenly perspective for those reading this right now. I pray you open their eyes to see your magnificence. Open their ears so they can hear you direct them and woo them into secret places and divine appointments. Give them supernatural faith to believe for the impossible, because nothing is impossible with you. Lord, let them never say, "This is too big." Instead, let them say, "This is so big it requires God, and I am going with him."

Lord, I see them singing in their wildernesses and you turning their songs into cries of war as they declare Psalm 108:1: "My heart, O God, is steadfast; I will sing and make music with all my soul." Lord, you form them into mighty warriors for the kingdom of God. They are yours, Lord, for you have written their names in the Lamb's Book of Life and on the palm of your hand. That is the very same hand that leads them through their wildernesses and their difficult places, and it's the hand that cradles them with never-ending love.

Thank you, Lord, for showing them step by step the path of their destiny and that they will not miss any opportunity you put before them to crush the enemy. I declare that they are the redeemed of the Lord, and they say so. Amen.

9. Expanding Influence

"Enlarge the place of your tent, stretch your tent curtains wide, do not hold back; lengthen your cords, strengthen your stakes." (Isaiah 54:2)

*N*ow that the Lord has fashioned us into weapons to take territory for him, he wants to expand and enlarge our sphere of influence for the kingdom of God.

The spirit of death threatened my community when Planned Parenthood announced their intentions to set up shop there. We were proud to have the largest metropolitan area without an abortion clinic, and we would guard the gates of our city so it stayed that way.

Just as the Lord commanded in Isaiah, we stretched our tent curtains, lengthened our cords, and strengthened our stakes by uniting a group of people from all walks of life. We called it Life and Family Coalition (L&FC). Our mission was to keep Planned Parenthood (PP) out of our community. I was asked to serve on the board and to be the media spokesperson for the organization.

We wrote a Sanctity of Life Proclamation, declaring that life begins at conception. Over two hundred thirty area-wide pastors signed it. We formed different factions within the coalition, including real estate agents for life, lawyers for life, and so on. We had no money, but we had passion.

The L&FC strategized ways to keep Planned Parenthood out and came up with several points of action. (1) We asked the city to pass ordinances for fetal disposal, informed consent, parental consent, and other protections. (2) We attended city council meetings to fight for an abortion-free community. (3) We created yard signs with "Stop Planned Parenthood" written on them and placed them in thousands of yards throughout the city. (4) We wrote letters to property owners and business owners, asking them not to rent or sell to PP. (5) We created an educational booklet filled with the signatures of thousands of people in our community who opposed plans for an abortion facility. (6) We paid to have that booklet inserted into our local newspaper.

Taking the Land

We did all we could to obstruct PP's plans, and our efforts had an effect. After we learned that PP wanted to buy a foreclosed building, we quickly got the word out and made phone calls. A generous attorney bought the building without even seeing it. He included a clause in the lease stating his refusal to do business with any abortion-related trade. Shortly after the purchase, he rented the building to a church that needed a new location. God's timing is so strategic.

Expanding Our Finances

One Sunday afternoon we gathered at a busy intersection and created a human life chain. We held hands and prayed for God to move in our city. As we finished up, a woman came over and handed me a bulging envelope. I thought it was filled with names for our signature ad, so I put it in my pocket, not thinking much about it.

After the rally, a few of our board members went for a bite to eat. Once we settled in at our table, I pulled the envelope from my pocket to see how many names were collected. I opened it and gasped. It wasn't stuffed with names — it was hundred dollar bills! We quickly slid out and counted the money. The cash totaled up to more than seventeen thousand dollars.

That was the first of many times we received envelopes of cash from that anonymous woman. Her generous contributions amounted to well over a hundred thousand dollars. We referred to her as our angel of life.

Victory from Praying in Our Tent

Planned Parenthood decided to locate in a different town within the Quad Cities area. They formed a straw man entity so they could anonymously purchase buildings or land. We again got word of their scheme and exposed them to the city council. The mayor at the time was pro-abortion but was angry about being deceived.

Finally, PP figured out a way to purchase land in that city. Landowners from outside the state, and with no vested interest in our community, sold them a plot. But we still had one fight left. The land they acquired didn't have the proper zoning for their use.

Again we prayed and prayed, this time specifically about that issue. Kathryn Bohn (another board member) and I felt an urge to borrow a motor home and place it across the street from Planned Parenthood's land. We fasted and prayed for twenty-one days in the motor home. Numerous people stopped by to pray with us and to donate money. Some buried Scriptures and crosses on PP's land, and many anointed it with oil, all the while declaring it as holy ground to be used for the purposes of God.

The adjacent property owners wrote letters to the city, stressing the importance of not rezoning the land for PP. Pro-life real estate agents did an appraisal study of other communities to learn the effects of abortion clinics on property values. The study proved that the presence of PP in a neighborhood diminishes market prices.

On the night the city council planned to make their rezoning decision, the chambers overflowed with concerned citizens. The crowds also filled the halls all the way to the entrance doors. Only a few PP supporters attended; the rest were pro-life residents.

The city voted "NO" to rezone the property, and instantly wild applause and screams of elation erupted. The irritated mayor pounded her gavel for order so the council could finish its business. Not ready to stop, we moved our loud celebration to the parking lot.

We joined in a circle and sang "Amazing Grace," praising the Lord for the victory he had just given us. Awed by our God of life, we shed tears of joy. The body of Christ had come together for an important purpose. We were so proud of them and of our city and its officials.

Months later, Planned Parenthood illegally sued the city at the federal level. Because the judge assigned to the case was a PP supporter, L&FC asked that he recuse himself. He refused and ruled in favor of PP. According to him, the city must rezone the land on the grounds that abortion is a constitutional right, which meant PP had a constitutional right to locate in the city.

We had several prayer vigils on the land across from PP's property. One of them happened in January in below-zero temperatures, and more than three thousand people attended. The community of believers united en masse while we fought to keep the death factory of Planned Parenthood out.

For six years we fought PP's proposed arrival, and we saw spectacular miracles of God during that time. Contractors refused to work on their construction. They had to go an hour away to find concrete. All the roadblocks the Lord helped us erect during those years delayed their efforts to build, ultimately costing them huge sums of money.

The Day God Cried with Us

On the day PP opened, their property swarmed with national media. Hundreds of pro-lifers with empty strollers showed up to pray, sing, and cry out to God. Rain fell the entire day, as if it was God's tears, and he was crying with us.

Our community refused to back down. Kathryn had the idea to organize a concert in the park next to the river to thank God for all he had done. We called it Praise for Life. Worship teams from local churches led us in praise all afternoon. We included dancers, flags, and banners. To top it off, our featured headliner was popular Christian music artist Kathy Troccoli. She had just written the song "Baby's Prayer"—confirmation that God handpicked her for the event.

The afternoon festivities were wonderful, and an estimated eight thousand people joined the celebration. However, the weather that day was hot and humid, and thunderstorms on the horizon threatened to ruin our party. We thought we might have to cancel Kathy's part.

Concerned for the safety of the crowd, we kept an eye on the radar, which showed storms all around the area. But directly above us the cloud mass parted, creating a hole of clear sky. It reunited as one giant force on the other side of the river.

Could it be that God had shown up with yet another miracle? Never before had we seen anything like it, and even the local weather forecasters expressed their surprise while reporting the phenomenon. We sat under starry skies and praised the Lord, while lightning and heavy rain across the river reminded us of God's amazing power.

God did not cry on Praise for Life night. His presence radiated brightly in those beautiful stars twinkling above us. What a memory and what an impact! After that, we invited Kathy

Troccoli to our area many other times to lead us in praise for what the Lord had done.

Stretching Our Tent Pegs and Influence

The landowner across the street from PP offered to sell L&FC a parcel of land for a reduced rate. We prayed and had a feasibility study done. We also talked with people in our community to get their opinions about the best use of the land and to see whether they would financially support it. The study showed people wanted a pregnancy center on the land directly across from PP. It also revealed that they were willing to back it. So we bought the land and began raising the money to build a center.

Our efforts brought completely different results from those of Planned Parenthood. Many contractors volunteered their services, and people gave generously to save babies and rescue women from a life of heartache and pain. By the time construction was finished, the building had two stories. The left side of the main floor housed the Women's Choice Center—a pregnancy center. To the right was a chapel where people could pray. A boardroom and community room made up the second floor. Bible studies, prayer groups, and other organizations could hold meetings in that room. It was our way of saying "thank you" to those who joined together to build it.

Governmental Stakes

The Lord taught us how important it is to stand for righteousness. We also realized the significance of having godly people in government to establish biblical and righteous laws. I felt a call to run for mayor of my city. I didn't win, but the Lord broke many fears and brought me to new levels of faith. I believe God also used that opportunity to form divine connections for future missions and to break strongholds over our city.

I got more involved in political campaigns to help elect Christian leaders. We opened our home to senate, congressional, and even presidential candidates, allowing them to come and share their ideas and policies. I was able to share my testimony and passion for the sanctity of life with them so they would know the truth about abortion. We prayed and prophesied over those candidates and many stayed in touch, asking for prayer as they faced opposition.

I had the privilege of meeting President George W. Bush. I thanked him for implementing policies defending life, and I shared my personal story of how abortion hurt me. Tears formed in his eyes as he listened. What a compassionate man! He hugged me, and I sensed he felt my pain. Later, after his speech to the enthusiastic crowd, he turned, caught my eye, and blew me a friendly kiss.

The Lord continued to open doors for me to speak and share my testimony. Not only did those opportunities bring more healing, but they also brought more influence and expanded my territory.

National Expansion and Influence

The Lord strengthened me in many areas. He taught me to hear him more clearly and to trust him in greater measure. I still love my quiet times with the Father. I enjoy listening to his heart and writing it all down.

One morning in my quiet time, the Lord nudged me to read an article in *Charisma Magazine* about an event being organized in Washington, D.C., by Jim and Anne Giminez. The leaders felt that seven giants were destroying our nation and needed to be pulled down. They called for millions to repent and ask God for mercy on our nation, crying out to God to deliver us from those giants. One of the giants was abortion.

They called the event Washington for Jesus, and it had been held two other times in the past. I was familiar with it because

Pat, Thelma, and I had gone in 1988. I asked the Lord how he wanted me to pray for it, and I sensed him say, "You will be speaking at this event to represent the sin of abortion."

"How is that going to happen, Lord?" I asked. "I don't know any of the event leaders. I'm just a nobody who lives in Iowa." The Lord brought it to my thoughts every day, and I finally concluded that the idea must really be from him. "Okay, Lord," I said. "I'll call the phone number given in the article, but to confirm it's really you, have Anna Giminez answer the phone."

I swallowed hard, dialed the number, and Anna Giminez answered. I shared my story and what the Lord had told me in prayer. She wanted me to come to D.C. and meet the team. And that was the beginning of a whirlwind of God moments and miracles.

Pat and I went to Washington and met with the organizers. They chose me to tell my testimony during the abortion segment of the event. Other speakers were Norma McCorvey, the Jane Roe of Roe v. Wade; Sydna Massey, who has a post-abortion ministry called Her Choice to Heal; and Nancy Alcorn, the founder of Mercy Ministries. The singing group Point of Grace provided the music. God had me on the ride of my life—slaying giants in the spiritual realm on the left and on the right.

When God Asks Us to Expand, He Provides

We had to provide our own transportation to D.C., so Pat arranged for a bus. That way we could take a large group. We notified the media, and they did a story about me—the local girl who would speak at a huge event in Washington.

En route to my Thursday night prayer group, I stopped at a store to pick up a few things. As I leaped out of my car, I saw a five dollar bill on the pavement by my tire. I picked it up and looked around for the possible owner, but I didn't see anyone. I put it in my purse and went into the store.

Once I arrived at the prayer group, I gave the five dollar bill to Ginny, another woman traveling to D.C. with us. I told her it was seed money for the trip. Ginny and I both needed two hundred fifty dollars—a total of five hundred dollars—for the bus trip to D.C., and we were trusting God for it. We set the five dollar bill on the floor and gathered in a circle around it. Ginny prayed that the Lord would multiply it a hundred fold and provide what we needed.

That Sunday, our church took up a special offering for a man named Vic Bally. Vic planned to go on a mission trip to Russia and was trusting God for the five hundred dollars still needed to meet his goal. Ginny donated our five dollar bill. After the offering was counted, Vic received the good news that God had answered his prayer. Contributions totaling five hundred dollars came in, covering his remaining expenses.

The story of my speaking in Washington appeared in our newspaper that following Monday. A local business owner called to say he saw the article and wanted to give toward the trip. He told me I could pick up a check for five hundred dollars that afternoon. I thanked him over and over and assured him I'd be there. As I finished the phone call, I looked up with a smile and said, "Really, Lord? You sent the exact amount. Thank you for providing!"

I called Ginny immediately. We screamed with delight over God's sweet surprise. When I picked up the check, I shared with that generous man the story of how God used him to answer a prayer.

Everything came together. The bus was full. Even my dad and his new wife, Cal, joined us. It would be the first time they heard my story.

Slaying the Giants

The drive to Washington seemed like one big church meeting on wheels. Our youth pastor brought his guitar, and we sang songs of worship and read the Word.

I opened my daily devotional to read that day's entry. It was about the giants we face in life and how God wants to use us as he did David to slay those giants. I couldn't contain my excitement. Of course I had to share it with everyone on the bus! It was another of God's many confirmations—another reminder that he was with us.

My friend Helen Corrao was on the bus and shared a prophetic word. She said, "The Lord gave me Jeremiah 1:5 for you." And then she spoke it over me. "I knew you before I formed you in your mother's womb. Before you were born I set you apart and appointed you a prophet to the nations." She prayed God would use my voice as a powerful prophetic weapon to destroy the sin of abortion in our nation. What she said pierced my heart, and I believed it was only the beginning of what God had in store. I placed that word—a precious, smooth stone—into my bag of weapons and revelations to carry into my destiny.

Hundreds of thousands came to the event to join in intercession for our nation. It was an awesome thing to see and experience. We first marched around the Capitol and blew the shofar, sounding the alarm for our nation to awaken and asking the Lord to forgive us for our sins.

Prayer and worship continued the rest of the day and throughout the night. Rain started to fall the next morning as we gathered to give testimony and repent for our sins. That was the Lord's way of showing us he heard our hearts. He wept with us while cleansing our nation with his tears.

As I stood on the stage and looked out at the crowd, I thought of the Lord's words: "One will put a thousand to flight, but two will put ten thousand to flight." All of the thousands of people in front of me were praying and worshipping, and I wondered how many thousands upon thousands were being put to flight.

God gave me a glimpse in my spirit of what was taking place in the heavens. I saw demons fleeing while the angels warred and rejoiced. We went back home physically exhausted but spiritually charged. The Lord was moving in our nation and in our community.

§

Things to Ponder

The Lord desires for you to expand your thinking and territory. He wants you to realize that he has great and mighty plans for you. Can you see how he has been forging you into a weapon that can be used to expand the kingdom of God? You are an instrument for uprooting and tearing down, for planting and building up. You are a giant slayer and a kingdom builder.

God has designed and created each of us with a purpose in mind. He has given us special gifts and passions. We often struggle with what our purpose is, and we spend more time trying to figure it out rather than walk it out.

I encourage you to expand your tent, lengthen your cords, and strengthen your stakes by digging deeper into the Word of the Lord and prayer. As you read your Bible, take each sentence and break it apart. Think of each word that is written, look up its meaning, and ask God why it is there or what he means by it. Listen carefully for his answer.

Many times we get in the routine of giving God our list of wants, and we tell him how we think he should do it. Yes, we ask him for things, but conversation and a relationship are built by listening as well. We should make time to listen to his desires and what he is revealing for us. "Therefore everyone who hears these words of mine and puts them into practice is like a wise man who built his house on the rock" (Matthew 7:24).

The second chapter of Proverbs is filled with the benefits of listening. "Tune your ears to wisdom, and concentrate on understanding. Cry out for insight, and ask for understanding. Search for them as you would for silver; seek them like hidden treasures. Then you will understand what it means to fear the LORD, and you will gain knowledge of God. For the LORD grants wisdom! From his mouth come knowledge and understanding" (Proverbs 2:2–6 NLT).

§

A Challenge

One word or touch from the Lord can change and transform us. In listening, we get our marching orders and direction from God. If we do only what our reasoning minds can think of, we can only go in our human strength and limits. But if we listen to God and walk in what he has for us, we will experience the supernatural, and there will be no limits.

I challenge you today to spend time listening to your maker and writing down what you hear. Then step into what he has said, and your life will be changed forever. You'll want to live in the extraordinary, being led by the Spirit of God. After you experience that, you will never want to return to the ordinary.

§

Prayer

Lord, thank you for speaking to these wonderful sisters and brothers of mine. I pray they will rise to new levels of faith and action with you. Reveal your amazing plans for them and expand their influence into new territories. Thank you for giving them ears to hear what your spirit is saying.

I declare over them that they will walk in the destiny for which you have created them and that they will have the vision to see your unlimited possibilities. Lord, I pray you break their hearts for the things that break yours and move them into action. Use them to rescue those who are broken and dying physically and spiritually. Give them boldness and remove all fear so they can walk in your ways all the days of their lives.

Bless them abundantly, Lord, and let them walk in truth and grace. Fill them with compassion and love. Let their lives reflect you always. I pray this in Jesus' name. Amen.

10. Influence for Generations

"You will spread out to the right and to the left; your descendants will dispossess nations and settle in their desolate cities." (Isaiah 54:3)

The Lord wants to spread you out to the right and to the left, far and wide. He has much for you to do. He has places to take you and truth he wants you to share. The Lord even has plans for your children and generations to come. You will teach them in the Lord, and they will remove giants from nations and take cities for the kingdom of God.

Wow! What an incredible promise he gave us. Are you seeing the wonderful plans he has for you and your family? Are you catching his vision and realizing your value and worth? You are a voice of truth for the Lord.

Expanding Our Voice for Truth

Ann and Nancy, a couple of my speaker friends, told me about an organization called Operation Outcry. The ministry was co-founded by Allan Parker, who also serves as president of The Justice Foundation. As an attorney, Allan's goal is to end abortion.

The Lord spoke to him through Isaiah 28:17–18, which says, "I will make justice the measuring line and righteousness the plumb line; hail will sweep away your refuge, the lie, and water will overflow your hiding place. Your covenant with death will be annulled; your agreement with the realm of the dead will not stand. When the overwhelming scourge sweeps by, you will be beaten down by it."

God gave Allan a clear message. "It is time for the covenant of death and the agreement with the grave made by our nation through the sin of abortion to end."

The Lord revealed three strategic pieces of evidence that could be given in a court case to overturn Roe v. Wade. One is the power of testimonies from women hurt by abortion. Allan created a declaration for women to fill out and sign. He hopes to present millions of these declarations to the Supreme Court when God's timing is right.

Through Operation Outcry, Allan is still collecting declarations as evidence to overturn Roe v. Wade, proving it is bad law and detrimental to our nation. If you are a woman hurt by abortion, you can let your voice be heard by signing one. The Moral Outcry is another organization collecting signatures from any citizens who want to see abortion end in our country.[9]

Operation Outcry had a conference in Dallas to educate women who wanted to be involved, so Nancy, Ann, Kathy Slinger (another friend), and I made the trip to Texas to see what the Lord was doing through this ministry. The Holy Spirit inspired each speaker, and we felt God work mightily. Because our hearts aligned with Allan's vision, we returned home and started an Iowa chapter of Operation Outcry, calling it Voice of Truth.

Government leaders and Christian organizations heard about Operation Outcry's concept. They invited us to speak

---

[9]   Discover how you can be involved in this historical movement at www. themoraloutcry.com or www.operationoutcry.org.

about the harm of abortion in their churches and to testify at state congressional hearings for pro-life legislation.

Spreading Out Across the World

Lou Engle organized a gathering for prayer and fasting on 07/07/07, known as The Call. It took place at Nissan Stadium (where the Tennessee Titans play) in Nashville.[10] Operation Outcry set up a tent in the stadium where they could minister to those hurt by abortion. Several of us from Iowa planned to go, and we reserved a block of hotel rooms. A friend of mine asked if we could share a room with Mary Jill, a woman attending from Hungary. We did and were excited to meet her.

Mary Jill was a delight and fit right in. On the last day of the event, I invited her to come back to Iowa with us. Before too long she sensed an answer in her spirit. "I'm going to Iowa," she said. We cheered and knew it was a God assignment.

As a missionary in Hungary, Mary Jill accomplished amazing things in that nation. She is post-abortive and wanted to see abortion recovery come to that part of the world, especially because of abortion's prevalence there.

Together we traveled across the country, speaking at events and taping television shows. Her visit was divinely ordered. Mary Jill requested that a couple of friends and I join her in Hungary, Serbia, and Ukraine to speak on the harm of abortion and to do trainings on abortion recovery. Never had I thought of doing something like that, but God is strategic and has huge plans beyond our imaginations.

Spiritually Dispossessing Nations

The organizers of an international pro-life conference in Israel invited representatives of Operation Outcry to speak.

---

[10] For more information on The Call, go to www.thecall.com.

Most of us had never been there, and it was a lifelong dream to step in the very places Jesus walked and taught. We took advantage of the opportunity and brought along our spouses and children. It was one of the most prayerful, powerful, and prophetic trips I have ever taken.

The Holy Spirit led us as we went to the Old Testament site of the Valley of Hinnom, where parents burned their children as a sacrifice to Baal and Molech. We cried and sobbed in repentance on behalf of those sins and of our own sin of sacrificing our children on the altar of convenience. We poured out pitchers of water representing the tears of Rachel, based on the words of Jeremiah 31:15. "A voice is heard in Ramah, mourning and great weeping, Rachel weeping for her children and refusing to be comforted, because they are no more."

We drove colored pencils with Scriptures on them into the ground, declaring that the Word of God would be the nation's foundation. The colored pencils served as representations and remembrances of our children. We blew shofars to sound the alarm to the enemy that we were taking back all he had stolen through the death of those children. As the shofar blew, it drowned out the Muslim call for prayer blasting from the nearby mosque. We rejoiced as the Lord confirmed that he is the one true God and he was pleased. We sang "Amazing Grace" loudly in the valley, and it echoed off the hills back to us, joining with the voices of angels.

We stood on the banks of the now dried stream to the Elah Valley where David slew Goliath the giant. We picked up five smooth stones as David did and stood in a line, naming the giants who had taunted us throughout our lives. And then we hurled our stones at those giants, declaring, "We come against you in the name of the Lord Almighty, the God of the armies of Israel, whom you have defied. This day the Lord will deliver you into our hands, and you are defeated." Our war cry added the exclamation point to our declaration. We knew we had victory through our God.

During the conference, we met so many wonderful believers from all over the world. We built friendships that opened doors for several of us to speak in other countries, including Holland, Dominican Republic, Philippines, Hungary, Syria, India, New Zealand, and many other places. We spoke at marches for life and talked with government officials about laws and the one-child policy. We helped start Operation Outcry ministries in their countries and did trainings for abortion recovery and healing.

God's Plans in India

The Lord had a divine appointment in Israel for Steve and me. We met Pastor Mohen Rao from India who had a vision to start one hundred churches in villages that had never heard the gospel. He wanted to expand a campus he built so they could house orphans and widows. He also wanted to add a Christian school to teach English and educate children so they would not have to live in poverty.

Our new pastor friend had already built ten churches, but because of opposition the tenth church had been burned down. Steve and I instantly connected with Pastor Mohen because of our love for India and our adoption of Zachary. Pastor Mohen said many times during the trip that he wanted to visit us in the United States. Just the potential of reuniting with him again filled us with joy.

The following summer, Pastor Mohen came to visit. I prayed for God's direction and arranged meetings with several pastors and ministry leaders. One of those meetings was with Pastor Tim Bowman. He is the founding pastor of Calvary Church of the Quad Cities where Steve and I attended for years. Pastor Tim has a heart for missions, so I knew this could be a divine appointment.

As we ate lunch that Friday, Pastor Mohen flipped through pages of books he brought. They were loaded with pictures of the people of India and the churches he built. He talked about his love for the Lord and the dreams God had given him. A stirring in my heart made me believe that Steve and I would one day go to India and experience what Pastor Mohen had shared. I had no idea what Pastor Tim was thinking or feeling.

Without warning, that Sunday at church Pastor Tim called Zachary up to the platform. He wrapped his arm around Zac and said, "Zachary, you are a precious gift from God to this congregation and to our nation. We are so thankful to God for the gift he has given us through you."

Pastor Tim went on to tell the congregation about Zac's adoption from India as well as the opportunities he and his wife, Cathy, were granted when they adopted their two boys. He turned and spoke directly to Zachary again. "In honor of you and our church's tenth anniversary, we as a body are going to rebuild the tenth church in India."

Applause erupted in the church, and tears of gratitude spilled down my cheeks. I closed my eyes to enjoy a quiet conversation with God. "Thank you, Lord, for such a wonderful gift. I would love to see my son preach in one of those churches someday."

This started a relationship with Pastor Mohen and the nation of India that none of us could have imagined. Calvary Church of the Quad Cities has helped build the kingdom of God and spread the gospel in many ways. As of this writing, Calvary has built twenty churches in India, bringing the total to twenty-nine.

Calvary has also purchased a school bus, built a second-story addition to the campus, and helped hire pastors to run each church that was built. The school has about five hundred students enrolled, and every one of them is being educated, fed, clothed, and taught the gospel of Jesus Christ.

To be a part of what the Lord is doing in India through Pastor Mohen's vision is such an honor. We, along with the Bowmans, have made several trips there to dedicate the church buildings and to experience the Lord's fruit through the beautiful Indian people.

God's Dreams Placed in Us

When God births a dream in us, he longs for us to step on the road of faith and bring it to fruition. He is the creator of the dream, and we are the vehicles used to bring it to pass.

The Old Testament book of Genesis tells us that God desired to save his chosen people Israel from starvation and extinction. Because of his plan to make them a great nation, he gave Joseph a dream. Joseph dreamt of bundles of wheat and the sun, moon, and stars bowing before him. It was God's revelation that Joseph would be a ruler one day.

However, Joseph's brothers weren't too keen on that news, and they treated him with disdain. They tore off the special robe his father had given him and threw him into a deep cistern to die. But when they realized they could sell him to traveling merchants and make some money, they pulled him out. He was carted off to Egypt — a foreign land with a foreign language — and sold into slavery.

From all appearances, Joseph's dream had been misinterpreted.

He spent time in a pit, became a servant in Potiphar's house, and was thrown in prison. It's not exactly what you'd expect when you're promised a leadership position. However, the Scriptures say that the Lord was with him on the entire journey.

Many years went by before Joseph saw the dream fulfilled. God promoted him to second in command to Pharaoh. He was in charge of the whole land of Egypt, including the supplies.

During a seven-year drought, his brothers traveled all the way from Canaan to Egypt to buy grain. They had the surprise of their life when they realized Joseph was the ruler, and they were terrified in his presence. Joseph noticed their fear and assured them. He said, "What you meant for evil God has used for good."

If we were Joseph's parents and knew that one day he'd be king, what would we do differently than God did? We'd probably send him to the finest colleges, dress him in expensive clothes, and give him favored treatment. But that's not the path God took for Joseph. God humbled Joseph and taught him to trust even in the worst of times.

In the book of First Samuel, we learn about God's dream to raise a prophet to save Israel. He planted that seed in a young, barren girl named Hannah, knowing all along that she would make good on her promise to return her child to him so he could rescue the godly line.

God also had a dream to save humanity from their sin and eternal damnation. He breathed his Holy Spirit upon a young virgin girl who said, "Yes, Lord, I am your servant. Let it be done to me according to your will." The power of the Most High overshadowed her. She carried the Son of God and birthed his plan of salvation for all mankind.

Mary aligned herself with God's dreams, and she pondered them in her heart. He used her in a mighty way, and she is now known and revered across the entire world and throughout history.

Likewise, God had a dream to save lost, hungry people in India. He placed a passion in Pastor Mohen's heart to start churches, a school, and a campus to house widows and orphans.

Keep this in mind: You are chosen of God and also carry the Lord in you. You are his passion and dream bearer. Listen closely for his voice. Will you also say yes and step into his miraculous story of making dreams come true?

I pray the Lord is stirring in your heart and reminding you of lost and forgotten dreams. He still wants to bring them to pass and reveal the great and mighty plans he has for you.

Dreams Redeemed

I had a dream of having children, and because of the natural consequences of what the abortion procedure did to my body, I thought that dream was lost. But it wasn't. God had a different plan. It was to build our family through the gift of adoption.

To redeem the loss of seeing the birth of my three children, the Lord allowed me to be in the delivery room to watch the arrival of three other children. I had the privilege of holding my sister Lynette's hand as we welcomed my nephew Caleb. I was invited to be in the room with my friend Tambi as she delivered her daughter, Adora. I also had the honor of being present with a friend, while her teen daughter went through the labor and delivery of her baby girl.

One day as I thanked God for such an incredible gift, he reminded me that the three children I lost were two girls and a boy—the same genders of the children I celebrated in the delivery room. Isn't the Lord amazing? He cares even about the small details of our lives and returns the moments we gave away in our deception.

God's Dreams for Zac

Today, I love witnessing God give dreams and visions to my son. Zac has grown up in a culture that values life. He realizes that God has a plan for each of our lives, and he knows that his is no exception.

When he was little, he would draw pictures of a building with a sign over it that read Living Water Center. I quizzed him about the pictures, and he said, "Mom, one day I am going to open an orphanage and medical center for children." What a big dream for such a little guy! I hid his words in my heart and prayed that the Lord would bring it about in his timing and in his way.

Zac seemed to have forgotten that vision, and as he got older, he didn't have clear direction of what he wanted to do with his life. He's creative and very social. He is a wonderful writer and has an eye for decorating. His smile extends the entire width of his face, and he brightens a room the moment he walks in. To Zachary, no one is a stranger, and when people meet him, they have an immediate connection. They say they feel as if they've known him forever.

When Zac told us he planned to join the military, Steve and I were shocked. That was so out of character for him. Even though I knew it was a noble call, I wasn't sure he heard God clearly. I was wrong. Zac joined the United States Air Force, and after basic training he worked in medical logistics and contracting. Through those assignments, the Lord was teaching Zac how to be disciplined, giving, and selfless, as well as showing him the administrative side of the medical field.

Zac was stationed at a hospital in San Antonio, Texas. He didn't know anyone, and it was his first time being away from home and family. Again God proved his faithfulness. Allan and Susan Parker, who founded The Justice Foundation and Operation Outcry, lived in San Antonio and took Zac under their wings. They invited him to church, welcomed him for Sunday dinners, and introduced him to people who would become instrumental in his life.

He got involved in church activities and helped with a big event called Night to Shine. It's a ministry Tim Tebow founded and is dedicated to ensuring that special needs children feel valued and loved. Zac loves children, especially special needs kids, and that made it a perfect fit. In the last couple of years, the Lord has reminded Zac of the dream he put in his heart when he was just a boy. Now Zac's hope is to work with orphanages and adoption agencies under the Tim Tebow Foundation and learn as the Lord brings clarity and direction to his dream.

In Zachary's Words

As my mom stated above, I didn't have a clear direction for my life. I was in school and not loving it. (Then again, who does?) I had a good friend, CPL Jason Pautsch, who was killed in Iraq in 2009 by a roadside bomb. In the days after that is when I felt something shift in my spirit.

I received a call from a recruiter with the Army, and I decided to take that step of faith and enlist. Thankfully, when I had announced to my parents that I was joining the military, they began to pray. Through their faithful prayers, I felt led to walk into to the Air Force recruiter's office—a choice I will never regret.

Leaving my parents' doorstep and entering the military was one of the hardest things I had experienced up until that point. It took a lot of prayers from so many. Those prayers carried me throughout my time in the Air Force and through two deployments to Afghanistan.

I struggled with depression during my first year in the military. I was constantly in tears, wishing and hoping that I could somehow get out of that legally binding contract and run home to my family. I would reach out to people back home and just cry with them. Suzette Jaques is one of those God-ordained friends. She would listen as I talked through my tears and then pray for me, encourage me, and, most importantly, love on me where I was. She had the ability to see my heart through my mess, and still does. She has been faithfully doing that for over a decade. If you don't have a "Suzette," I encourage you to find one. Your life will never be the same.

During that time, God was working on my heart and strengthening me. I received a message from one of my youth leaders, Shawna Partlow, and the message said, "Our lives are like film—we are developed in the dark places, and out of the darkness true beauty arises!" In that moment, I fell to my knees and said to the Lord, "I promise I will serve you all the days of my life. I need you. I have been trying to make it on my own, and my heart hasn't been positioned toward you, ready and willing to receive all that you have for me."

Spreading to the Right and Left

Within less than a week of my prayer, I found courage to attend the young adult service at Community Bible Church. During that service, I met my best friend, Luis Churion, who became influential in my life. He was—and still is—one of my biggest prayer warriors, and he introduced me to a world of people. I often think of those moments as a kiss from heaven. For the first time in what seemed like forever, I felt like I was in the Lord's plan, walking with him hand in hand.

I have literally taken the longest way possible to fulfill the calling God placed on my life: to open an adoption agency/ orphanage and medical center. I do believe that there are no mistakes and that my journey only made me stronger and more pliable for him to work. I recently returned home from my last deployment to Afghanistan, and while I was there, I continued to hear God call me. "Now is the time. Hang up the uniform, and chase after me. Run after the dreams I have given you." My heart's desire is to truly live out James 1:27 and to "look after the orphans in their distress."

Having a front row seat to the pro-life movement, it is no surprise I want to help overturn Roe v. Wade. I pray abortion ends and the alternative option of adoption grows. I want to focus on infants who have been abandoned at a fire or police station through the Safe Haven law. I would love to defy odds by encouraging families to adopt older children, as—according to statistics—children over the age of five are much harder to adopt and are more likely to end up getting shuffled around the foster care system.

My work with Night to Shine has drawn me into the special needs community. I would love to find those amazing families who are willing to help mend hearts, develop lives, and create forever families.

Some may look at my story and see someone who was destined for nothing more than what the orphanage had to offer. I look at my story and see God. I see the heart of our Father, a heart that pursues his beloved. I see passion. I see love. Most of all, I see forgiveness. I have often been asked if I want to meet my birth parents. Have I ever wondered who they are? I will say this: Yes. Yes, I want to meet them and say thank you. Thank you for being selfless and letting me go so God could use my life to heal someone's past, to show them what grace and forgiveness really look like. I would say thank you for loving me enough to give me an opportunity at life and, more importantly, a relationship with Jesus.

During my human moments when I feel I am inadequate or not educated enough to fulfill the calling, God bends down and continues to give me those kisses from heaven. Recently, as I was out-processing from the military, I sat down to have breakfast with someone I barely knew. He asked me what I was going to do post-military. I shared my story on adoption and that I wanted to build an adoption agency. He told me, "I know one person who does foreign adoptions and has worked with orphanages in India. He is based out of St. Louis, Missouri."

I replied, "Is his name Frank Block?" Frank Block was the executive director of the Love Basket Adoption Agency in Hillsboro, Missouri. He was the man who directed my adoption and placed me with my forever family. The young man I was having breakfast with had dated his daughter for years.

What are the odds that all the way in San Antonio, Texas, God would still be connecting me with someone from so many years ago? But God . . . It was a beautiful kiss from heaven yet again. Often when I feel doubt or let fear creep in, I get those kisses from heaven. Some are so small, but to me they're just confirmation that I am following his will.

§

Questions to Ponder from Zac

Do you feel like you have missed the mark? Have you taken the longest route possible to fulfill your dream? Don't give up. He gave you that dream for a reason. He wants to shape history through you. He wants you to influence generations to come for the kingdom of God.

When you feel alone or defeated, look for those sweet kisses from heaven, embrace the journey, and let God rewrite your story.

Let this verse encourage you today. "'For I know the plans I have for you,' declares the LORD, 'plans to prosper you and not to harm you, plans to give you hope and a future'" (Jeremiah 29:11).

11. The Heritage

"No weapon forged against you will prevail, and you will refute every tongue that accuses you. This is the heritage of the servants of the LORD, and this is their vindication from me," declares the LORD. (Isaiah 54:17)

The verse above is profound and carries a promise from our Lord that he will always vindicate us. He will not let the plans and strategies of the enemy come against us or succeed. He even promises that when people speak against us, their lies will be discredited. He is our defender, our vindicator, and our advocate. This is our heritage when we are his. What a remarkable promise! We have his word on this, so what do we have to fear? If God is for us, who can be against us?

The Lord assures us that we can go for it. He has our backs; the sky is the limit. We need to trust him when he says nothing is too difficult for him—and when we are in him, nothing is impossible for us.

When we believe what the Word of God says, it causes us to step out into places of faith. When we step out in faith, we are awed and amazed by the greatness of our mighty God.

Wholeness Is Our Inheritance

Being a part of the Lord's plans and knowing that it's our heritage and legacy is mind blowing. He works in supernatural ways to bring vindication for the things the enemy stole from us.

The Lord desires to use our past as a rich heritage for our future. We may see pain and devastation, but the Lord sees our character, strength, and ability to trust him that he developed in us through those hard seasons of our lives. He uses the trials as stepping stones to build our inheritance.

Psalm 1:1–3 gives us encouragement in that regard. "Oh, the joys of those who do not follow the advice of the wicked, or stand around with sinners, or join in with mockers. But they delight in the law of the LORD, meditating on it day and night. They are like trees planted along the riverbank, bearing fruit each season. Their leaves never wither, and they prosper in all they do" (NLT).

As we learn to rejoice and wait on the Lord in the hard times, we grow and mature. That process brings freedom not only to us but also to our family line. When we gain victory, it spills over into our children's lives and to generations to come. In the same way, when we live under certain sins and bondages, our children inherit those for generations.

Let's walk with God and trust him on our life path so we and our family line can enjoy all his benefits for generations to come.

Taking Back What the Enemy Stole

God blessed me on two particular occasions with special experiences I now treasure in my heart. I received an invitation to speak at an all school assembly at the high school I attended. Because I got pregnant my sophomore year, I didn't graduate. The organization asked me to talk about the failure that caused me to leave that place.

Even though the task seemed daunting, the Lord used that high school speaking opportunity as a place of restoration for me. He bound up broken hearts and set captives free from the lie of promiscuity through my testimony.

God gave me the chance of a lifetime, and it meant so much to me. My plan was to open my mouth wide and shatter the lies the enemy continued to tell those young people about sex. I shared how valuable they were to God and emphasized that they were worth more than giving themselves away. I told them that sex isn't love because love doesn't demand its own way. Love waits. Sex is a bond and covenant between two people who are committed to marriage.

I felt as if the Lord allowed me to take my foot—which was shod with the gospel of peace—and stomp on the neck of the enemy who had lied to me and was now lying to those kids. I then pulled a smooth stone from my pouch and planted it forcefully into his head. And I did it in the very place he had defeated me years ago. Take that, devil! Yes, God is the God of restoration.

The Lord also blessed me with an invitation to be the keynote speaker for the Pregnancy Resource Center's annual banquet in my hometown. Many of the people in the audience had grown up with me and gone to the same schools. They knew the Luana of the past but not the Luana of the present.

My brother, Larry, and his wife, Cindy, sat at a table their church had sponsored. They both knew my life had changed, but we lived in different cities, so they weren't able to see who I had become. Linda and my husband, Steve, sat at the table with me. Their job was to pray. I invited Dad and my stepmom, Cal, and they sat at a table in the front with some of their friends. My dad had not heard my whole story.

I was nervous. My family was in the audience, and I knew many others in the crowd. I thought about the woman in the Bible who had been brought to Jesus to be stoned because of her sin. Would people throw stones of judgment at me? Would they question my transformation?

I spent time in prayer, talking to God about my concerns and asking him to calm my spirit. The Lord wrapped me in his sweet peace and comforted me with his love. He reminded me of my mission. "Luana, this isn't about you. It's about giving me glory and enlightening people about the destruction of abortion."

My job was to talk about Jesus and his desire to save and heal. I was there to educate people and to help their hearts change. And I hoped they would donate lots of money to a worthy cause for life.

My preparation time for the event was so profound and restorative. The Lord had given me a revelation about honoring my dad. On our way to the banquet, I purchased a bouquet of flowers, and as I told my story that night, I introduced my father and asked him to stand. Steve presented the flowers to him while I thanked him and told him I loved him. The crowd rose to their feet to give him a standing ovation. There wasn't a dry eye in the room.

I'm grateful to God for that monumental moment. He allowed me to honor my dad and to publicly tell him I love him. The Lord also gave me the opportunity to publicly testify of his redeeming love to those who witnessed my past life of sin and destruction. All my fears of rejection and condemnation from the crowd were lies from the enemy. Everyone treated me with compassion and loving-kindness.

I'm in awe of how God cares about every detail of our lives. He even transforms our story into his story. The experiences he gives us far exceed anything we could imagine. My wonderful Lord never ceases to amaze me.

Ask for Nations as Your Inheritance

The Lord's perspective is so much grander than ours. When he says, "This is the heritage of the servants of the Lord," he sees a larger scope. He sees you and your family line. He also sees your nation.

In Psalm 2:7–8, the king proclaims the Lord's decree. Take note of what he says about our inheritance: "The LORD said to me, 'You are my son. Today I have become your Father. Only ask, and I will give you the nations as your inheritance, the whole earth as your possession'" (NLT).

Do you have enough faith, and are you bold enough to believe God will give you your nation as your inheritance?

The Lord gave me an extraordinary opportunity to testify before a congressional judiciary committee hearing in Washington, D.C. My purpose was to bring evidence that Planned Parenthood should no longer be funded by federal tax dollars. Not only was I honored to testify, I also considered it as part of my inheritance. My constant prayer is that our nation will no longer be under a covenant of death, but that we will annul and break that covenant and become a nation that promotes a culture of life.

The Lord revealed himself continually throughout my entire time in D.C. I could fill an entire book writing about all he did, but for now I'll encourage you by sharing a few of the miracles.

When I found out that I was chosen to testify, I was apprehensive. Given only five minutes to speak, I wanted to make sure every word counted. It was important for me to have a powerful message and to be in tune with the Holy Spirit. The committee needed to understand the destruction of abortion, not just to the babies but also to the women. I hoped their hearts would change and that funding for this sin would end.

As I prepared, the Lord spoke to me through three different passages of Scripture. First, God reminded me of Jeremiah 1:5–10:

"I knew you before I formed you in your mother's womb. Before you were born I set you apart and appointed you as my prophet to the nations."

"O Sovereign LORD," I said, "I can't speak for you! I'm too young!"

The LORD replied, "Don't say, 'I'm too young,' for you must go wherever I send you and say whatever I tell you. And don't be afraid of the people, for I will be with you and will protect you. I, the LORD, have spoken!" Then the LORD reached out and touched my mouth and said,

"Look, I have put my words in your mouth! Today I appoint you to stand up against nations and kingdoms. Some you must uproot and tear down, destroy and overthrow. Others you must build up and plant." (NLT)

I knew God had given me a mission and that he would be with me and lead me.

The Lord also told me to read and declare Psalm 46. So I read it and proclaimed it over the hearing.

God is our refuge and strength, always ready to help in times of trouble. So we will not fear when earthquakes come and the mountains crumble into the sea. Let the oceans roar and foam. Let the mountains tremble as the waters surge!

A river brings joy to the city of our God, the sacred home of the Most High. God dwells in that city; it cannot be destroyed. From the very break of day, God will protect it. The nations are in chaos, and their kingdoms crumble! God's voice thunders, and the earth melts! The LORD of Heaven's Armies is here among us; the God of Israel is our fortress.

Come, see the glorious works of the LORD: See how he brings destruction upon the world. He causes wars to end throughout the earth. He breaks the bow and snaps the spear; he burns the shields with fire.

"Be still, and know that I am God! I will be honored by every nation. I will be honored throughout the world."

The LORD of Heaven's Armies is here among us; the God of Israel is our fortress. (NLT)

When I got to verse ten, God said, "Now be still and know that I am God! I will be with you as you speak this. I arranged it, and I have no intention of leaving you alone in it." Every time I felt frightened or anxious, I heard him whisper, "Be still and know that I am God. I have this."

Todd Williams, a friend of mine, also shared Mark 13:9–11 with me to give encouragement. I felt it was a direct word from the Lord, so I stood on that Scripture and prayed it over the hearing as well. Part of it says, "You will stand trial before governors and kings because you are my followers, but this will be your opportunity to tell them about me . . . for it is not you who will be speaking but the Holy Spirit."

Seeing Miracles and Hearing God Speak

My friend Alanna McGovern accompanied me on the trip to be a prayer support. We connected with Allan Parker when we arrived and then met for prayer at Dick Simmons's home, which is located right behind the Supreme Court. After a powerful time of prayer, we decided to go to David's Tent located on the National Mall.

The tent had been put up a couple of months prior and was there for 24/7 praise, worship, and prayer for our nation. As we walked, we realized we might have farther to go than we thought, so we hailed a taxi. One pulled up behind us, but two ladies had already snagged it. We expressed our need for a ride, and they offered to share their taxi. We accepted and jumped in.

The women asked us if we lived in D.C. or were visiting. As we grew deeper in conversation, we discovered that they were attorneys and lobbyists for Planned Parenthood. I couldn't help but laugh. My eyes turned to heaven, and I silently asked the Lord what he was up to with this divine appointment. I knew the odds were slim to none that in a city the size of Washington, five people from opposite views would be placed in a small space together.

Suddenly, I heard the Lord say, "They are not your enemy. You do not war against flesh and blood but against principalities, against powers, against the rulers of the darkness of this world, and against spiritual wickedness in high places. I love them." My heart filled with a compassionate love for them as the Lord spoke that word.

We talked about our reasons for being there and said it would be good to see familiar faces in the hearing room. When we reached our destination, they paid for the taxi, stating that we were on their way. The three of us stood on the sidewalk as they drove away and prayed for each of them. We asked the Lord to break the power of the lie they believed and to reveal his truth to them. We declared that this was the day of their salvation. I still continue to pray for those two beautiful ladies.

More Divine Assignments

We walked to David's Tent, marveling at what the Lord had just done and what he would continue to do. In David's Tent, a couple there from San Antonio, Texas, knew Allan. They said they just arrived in town. The Lord told them he had an assignment for them in D.C., so they dropped everything and came. When they saw Allan, they knew their assignment was to pray for us and what the Lord wanted accomplished. They stayed with us throughout the entire trip, praying for God's will to be done.

I marvel at how the Lord went ahead of us long before we got there and put things in order. We also met Jason Hershey, the man who received the vision from the Lord to erect David's Tent. I encourage you to read his powerful God story.[11]

The next morning, Alanna and I prayed. We left our Bibles opened to Jeremiah 1 and Psalm 46 as we went down to the lobby to meet Allan and pray for the hearing. We were pleasantly surprised to see Matt Lockett, Paige Cofield, and Josh Shepherd from Justice House of Prayer (JHOP) waiting with Allan in the lobby.[12]

We sat around a large table in a side room and took turns praying. Paige said a Scripture kept coming to her mind, and she wanted to read it. As she read Psalm 46 out loud, she stopped at verse ten and said to me, "The Lord is saying, 'Be still and know he is God; he is with you.' He wants you to know he's got this. He planned and arranged it all." I felt the tears well up in my eyes. She finished the passage and we continued praying.

---

[11] www.davidstentdc.org

[12] www.jhopdc.com

Then Josh turned to Jeremiah 1:5–10 and declared it out loud, saying God was speaking this word. A sense of holy awe fell over Alanna and me as we thought about our intimate and personal God. Even more tears slid down my face. We hadn't told any of them about the Scriptures the Lord had given me ahead of time.

We continued praying, and Matt kept receiving the message in Mark 13:9–11, so he spoke it in his prayers. By that time, I was completely undone by God's goodness and kindness. He confirmed again and again that he indeed was present and at work. That day was preordained in the spiritual realm for our nation and for his glory.

We arrived at the hearing room an hour early, so we prayed over every chair and for all those who would fill the chairs. We broke the power of darkness and asked the Lord to rush in with his mighty truth and light.

Three of us would testify for life—Dr. Levatino (a former abortionist), Sue Thayer (a former manager of a Planned Parenthood), and me. A lawyer, arguing on Planned Parenthood's behalf, would also speak. Many prayer warriors filled seats in the room, and I could feel the effects of their prayers. God was present and active, shifting the atmosphere and changing mindsets.

A timer placed in front of us buzzed when our allotted five minutes was up, at which point our microphones turned off. Watching the timer unnerved me, so I prayed and focused on the congressmen. I told my story of how abortion caused devastation, addiction, and infertility in my life.

Thousands of declarations signed by women who had been hurt by abortion were stacked in front of me. Not only was I representing myself, but I was also testifying on behalf of those wounded women and their aborted children. I felt the weight and holiness of it. I wanted those committee members to know that abortion is not healthcare but a death sentence for women and babies. Funding Planned Parenthood with tax dollars forces those of us who were hurt by abortion to pay our abusers.

Complete silence permeated the room as I spoke. After I finished, Allan put his hand on my shoulder and whispered in my ear, "You went over your five minutes." I looked at my timer. It had counted backwards but never buzzed, and my microphone never shut off.

Standing on God's Promises

We had dinner with Matt Lockett and the JHOP team after the hearing finished. It was a wonderful time of fellowship and hearing about the miracles God had performed for, and through, the Justice House of Prayer. We closed out the evening by placing Allan's rod of justice on the center of the long table. With all of our hands around it, we held it high as we prayed. The Lord gave us Scriptures and powerful prophetic words.

As I held the rod, I felt leaves budding. I opened my eyes several times but didn't see anything. I knew then that God was showing me something in the Spirit. I saw an almond branch budding. I didn't know how to interpret my vision, so I stayed silent. Several minutes later the picture still hadn't left my mind. I decided to speak up, and I shared what I had seen and felt.

Matt asked, "Luana, what do you see budding? Is it the rod we are holding or an almond branch?" I explained that I saw an almond branch in my mind. Matt got excited and said, "The rest of the Jeremiah 1 passage the Lord gave you talks about that."

Here's what it says in verses eleven and twelve:

> Then the LORD said to me, "Look, Jeremiah! What do you see?"
>
> And I replied, "I see a branch from an almond tree."

145

> And the LORD said, "That's right, and it means
> that I am watching, and I will certainly carry out
> all my plans." (NLT)

Matt continued, "That means the Lord will carry out his plan to defund and end abortion in our land." We were elated and again gave praise and honor to the Lord.

The Soil Is Polluted

Matt told us the National Mall was under construction. They had tried to grow grass, but no matter what they did it wouldn't grow. First they seeded the ground, but it didn't grow. Then they laid sod, but it didn't adhere to the ground or grow. After all their attempts failed, the city hired an expert to do an analysis on the soil.

The report stated that the soil was polluted from everything that had taken place on it over the years. To get the grass to grow, they would have to dig twenty-two feet and put in a new foundation of dirt. It was a natural manifestation of what was happening spiritually in our nation. We prayed that as the National Mall received a new foundation our nation would return to her Christian foundation and re-dig the wells of revival.

The next day, Alanna and I prayed as we walked around the Capitol, the National Mall, and some of the other memorials. We saw where they were digging, so we stopped to pray. As we did that, I saw in my spirit a picture of us throwing seeds into the newly turned dirt. I looked at Alanna and said, "I wish we had some seeds."

She let out a screech and said, "I do! The Lord told me to bring mustard seeds." She gently pulled out a baggie of the mustard seeds she carefully packed before we came to D.C.

Again we were overjoyed at God's plans and for allowing us to be a part of his purposes. How cool that God told Alanna to specifically bring mustard seeds, for the Lord says in his

Word we need faith only the size of a mustard seed to move a mountain and change our situation.

We threw those mustard seeds of faith into the newly turned dirt and declared that our nation will again be a nation who has faith in the Lord Jesus Christ. We are one nation, under God, indivisible, with liberty and justice for all.

Months later a bill to defund Planned Parenthood passed the senate and house but was vetoed by President Obama. We will continue to stand on the promises of God and declare that we are a nation of life, freedom, and justice for all, because that is our heritage from the Lord.

Promises Fulfilled

God is a God of his promises. Two weeks ago as of this writing, Planned Parenthood announced that they would be closing several clinics across the United States. Four of the soon-to-be-closed clinics are in Iowa. That will leave only eight Planned Parenthood facilities in the state of Iowa where children can be killed. But eight is eight too many. We pray for the day every child will be valued and allowed to live.

One of the facilities closing is the one we tried so hard to keep out. Oh yes, God is a promise keeper. He answers prayers and reveals his power daily if we pray and believe.

§

Application

We've been on an incredible journey together. My prayer for you is that you will have received deposits and revelations from the Lord throughout this book, making you stronger and even more in love with your amazing Savior, friend, and deliverer. Here's one thing specifically I want you to remember: you are a priceless treasure of the Lord, and he loves you so much.

I pray you sing and even dance through all your wildernesses and barren places in life. May the Lord turn them into well-watered valleys that produce much fruit.

I declare over you that you are a mighty weapon of mass destruction in the hands of the Lord that will hit the mark every time, take down the enemy, and set captives free. Ask God about the plans he has for you and get involved in ministry.

Is he calling you to work at a Pregnancy Resource Center? Does he want you to lead an abortion recovery group? Will you be a voice for the voiceless? Is he asking you to lead a prayer group or a Bible study? Have you been set free from addiction and called to minister to others trapped in that same bondage?

With the Lord ALL things are possible for you, so dream big and often. The Lord has places for you to go and things for you to do that you cannot even imagine. Pursue your passions. God put them in you to help others. Ask the Lord what your ministry looks like and how to begin. He already has the plan all laid out.

Always forgive, and always ask for forgiveness quickly, and your heart will be filled with love that is plentiful and true. In turn you will be loved in great measure. God has spectacular plans for all of us. We can only dream of the places he wants to take us and the things he wants to show us.

We are all on this journey and in the process of being honed, pruned, and sharpened to be his weapons of warfare, his songs of worship, and his heritage and legacy. All you have to do is listen for his voice and then step into what he is showing you.

I can't wait to hear from you as you experience what God has for you. If you are hurting and want prayer, or are excited to share what God is doing, I would be honored to pray with you. Please contact me at Luana.R.Stoltenberg@gmail.com.

Here are a few questions for you to ponder:

How will you walk this journey? Will you rescue those who are unjustly sentenced to die, saving them before they stagger to their [spiritual or physical] death? (See Proverbs 24:11.) Will you sing in the wilderness?

§

Prayer

Lord, thank you for these precious saints. I declare the promises of God over them. Give them courage and boldness to stand. Let them be vessels of honor and weapons that are mighty in your hand. I pray faithfulness over them. Let them not grow weary in well doing but cling tightly to you and the purposes you have created them for. I speak promotion and prosperity over them. Lord, I thank you that you go before them, you walk beside them, and you are their rear guard. The joy of the Lord is their strength as they venture through the wilderness and mountain tops because you are always with them. I ask all this in Jesus' name. Amen.

About the Author

Luana has been involved in the pro-life movement since 1987. She is an international speaker and has taught abortion recovery groups and other Bible studies.

She is the vice president of The Pregnancy Resource Centers in the Quad Cities. She is on the advisory board for Operation Outcry, and is also a part of several other boards. Luana was part of the founding board of The Women's Choice Center in Bettendorf, Iowa.

Luana has been married to Steve since 1985, and they live in Davenport, Iowa. They have one child, Zachary, who is adopted from India.

Luana's heart is to show the love and mercy of Christ, by telling people how the Lord picked her up from a life of drugs, alcohol, and abortions, and placed her on his lap of grace. She loves to pray, attend Bible studies, take long walks, ride horses, and relax on the beach.

To connect with Luana or to schedule a speaking engagement:
Luana Stoltenberg
www.Luanastoltenberg.com
Luana.r.stoltenberg@gmail.com

CPSIA information can be obtained
at www.ICGtesting.com
Printed in the USA
BVHW04s1519250618
519964BV00030B/1686/P